D0712090

CHESS IS MY LIFE

Chess is my Life

Autobiography and Games

Victor Korchnoi

Translated by Ken Neat

Arco Publishing Company, Inc. *New York*

First published 1978
© Viktor Korchnoi 1978
ISBN 0–668–044528–0
LCCN 77–17659

Published 1978 by
Arco Publishing Company Inc.
219 Park Avenue South
New York N.Y. 10003

Printed in Great Britain

Contents

Career Record 1947–1976

Born Leningrad July 23, 1931

USSR Junior Championships
1947 1st
1948 1st =

USSR Championships
27th	1960	1st
30th	1962	1st
32nd	1964/65	1st
38th	1970	1st

World Championship Series
Candidates 1962
Candidates 1968
$\frac{1}{4}$ final beat Reshevsky 5$\frac{1}{2}$–2$\frac{1}{2}$
$\frac{1}{2}$ final beat Tal 5$\frac{1}{2}$–4$\frac{1}{2}$
final lost Spassky 3$\frac{1}{2}$–6$\frac{1}{2}$
Candidates 1971
$\frac{1}{4}$ final beat Geller 5$\frac{1}{2}$–2$\frac{1}{2}$
$\frac{1}{2}$ final lost Petrosian 4$\frac{1}{2}$–5$\frac{1}{2}$

Candidates 1974
$\frac{1}{4}$ final beat Mecking 7$\frac{1}{2}$–5$\frac{1}{2}$
$\frac{1}{2}$ final beat Petrosian 3$\frac{1}{2}$–1$\frac{1}{2}$
final lost Karpov 11$\frac{1}{2}$–12$\frac{1}{2}$

International Tournament
Firsts include:
Bucuresti 1954
Hastings 1955–56 (1st. =)
Buenos Aires 1960
Budapest 1963
Havana 1963
Erevan 1965
Gyula 1965 (14$\frac{1}{2}$–$\frac{1}{2}$)
Sochi 1966
Palma de Mallorca 1968
Sarajevo 1968
Lukacovica 1969
Wijk aan Zee 1971
Hastings 1971–72 (1st =)
Interzonal 1973
Amsterdam 1976 (1st =)

* 1 *

Childhood Years

In the picturesque streets of the town of Palma de Majorca, I once met a man who spoke excellent Russian, with a lordly, aristocratic accent. On making his acquaintance, I soon learned that he could trace his genealogical line back to the sixteenth century – he reckoned that one of his ancestors was Andrey Staritsky, who had stirred up a rebellion against Ivan the Terrible. Such a man is to be envied. Leaning on his ancestors, a man acquires self-confidence, and a pride in himself, and his responsibility to them expresses itself in a need to assimilate the culture of mankind.

In our times, when wars alternate with revolutions, few can boast of a deep genealogical past. I am particularly unfortunate; I didn't even know my grandfathers. One of them, I heard, was a nobleman of Ukrainian ancestry, the other spent his whole life in a small Jewish town near Kiev. I had only a grandmother, Polish by nationality, and I spent the first ten years of my life with her.

I was born in 1931, during the first Stalin Five-Year Plan. My parents were poor, but there was nothing unusual about this: at that time there were frequent purges, and particular attention was paid to purging the purses of the population – with the aim, of course, of achieving genuine equality for all people. In this respect the authorities were highly successful: on the eve of the war there were tens of millions of people living in poverty.

Things weren't easy for me. My mother was a woman of eccentric character, and our family broke up rather quickly. She was very poor, and it soon became impossible for her to feed me and bring me up, and so she handed me over to my father and his household. My mother was a pianist, and had completed a course at the Conservatoire, but her poverty staggered me: for decades of her working life she was unable to acquire any normal furniture. Her room contained nothing but the barest essentials — a bed, chair, stool, cupboard and a fragment of mirror. All her life her piano was rented. Later, on dozens of occasions, I was to hear from her lips the event that had become the tragedy of her life — she had nothing with which to feed me, and had been forced to give me away.

I ended up with my father's relations. They were of the Polish nobility, and had previously been rich, but the new regime had succeeded in making everyone equal before God and Stalin. However, I recall old furniture, fine books, and conversations which touched on questions other than that of how to feed the family during the coming months. I was baptized a Catholic, and my grandmother saw to it that I observed the accepted practices.

My father was a teacher of Russian Language and Literature, and was also a Refrigeration Engineer, and worked at a confectionary factory. There, at the factory, he met a woman who was later to become his wife and my stepmother, and after his death she continued (as she does to this day) to take care of me as if I were her own son.

My father gave serious consideration to my education, and although at home every kopeck had to be counted, since there were no savings or anything to spare, he found it possible to engage a teacher to give me lessons at home in German, at the same time as my first years of learning at school.

I learned to play chess somewhere around the age of six. My father taught me, and I enjoyed playing with him, with his brother, and with all members of the family. They sensed my need to play, and I remember my uncle saying to me: 'If you won't speak Polish, then I won't play chess with you!' But there was as yet no serious interest, we didn't have even one chess book. We followed certain events, and sometimes in a children's magazine we would find a chess section with a game. That was all. I only became keen on chess much later, in adolescence, towards the end of the war.

In the terrible year of 1941, I reached my tenth birthday. Children from Leningrad schools were evacuated by the government deep into the country, and my father supported this idea. I set off with my class-mates 'on evacuation' as it was then called. In the confusion of the outbreak of war, I had an unusual journey. Our school was held up, somewhere for a long time about 300 kilometres from Leningrad. My mother, whom I used to see occasionally, became alarmed when she learned that we had been held up. On hearing that certain special school trains had been bombed while en route, she came rushing along to save me, and took me back with her. Having lost all our possessions on the way when one of the stations was being bombed, we somehow returned to Leningrad which is where I spent the whole of the war years.

At the beginning of the war a rationing system was introduced. With each succeeding month the rations were cut more and more, until they reached the level which made active life impossible. Had it not been for the death of my relations – from hunger and deprivation – I doubt whether I would have managed to survive.

I lived in an enormous thirteen-roomed communal flat, where eleven families were huddled together. My first steps, and then my first bicycle rides, were in the enormous fifty-metre corridor which connected the tenants. When the war commenced, the flat began to empty. Some went away, and those remaining started to die one by one of hunger. My father was sent to the front early in November 1941, and, as I later learned, was killed in one of the first battles, on the banks of Lake Ladoga. My uncle disappeared even sooner, and of his fate I know nothing. Then within a couple of months I was burying my grandmother and her brother. Our neighbour and I would wrap the corpse in a sheet, lie it on a sledge, and drag it right across town to the cemetery. But the ration cards of the deceased remained – until the end of the month, and sometimes for a month after that. The dead lent the living a helping hand!

I was also helped by my stepmother. From time to time she managed to take me to her factory, where she would feed me up on spice cake and pastries. The devil only knows what they were made of, it was not ordinary flour, but they were still fairly substantial. Despite this, at the end of 1942 I had to go into hospital suffering from dystrophy.

The most difficult days of the blockade were during the winter of 1941–42. It was cold, there was no firewood to light the stove, the water supply and sewerage system were not working, and the trains weren't running. At one point – in January and February – even the newspapers failed to appear. The Leningrad radio station operated intermittently. I remember how I would set off to the Nyeva carrying two buckets, with difficulty reach the water in the ice-holes, which were frozen round the edges, and then with full buckets walk a kilometre and a half back home. I used to go to the shops for provisions, and sometimes my grandmother would send me to the market to exchange bread for firewood for our small home-made stove.

When my grandma died, I settled down completely in my stepmother's house. Starting in the autumn of 1942 the schools once again began to function, and in September I restarted in the fifth year. I didn't learn very well, for I was insufficiently careful, but on the other hand I was ambitious, and if I set myself some task, then I would accomplish it.

* 2 *

Chess Alone

At the end of 1943 the war situation near Leningrad began to improve. The blockade was finally broken. Notices appeared in the schools, appealing for us to enrole in the Pioneers' Palaces.

At this point I should explain that throughout the Soviet Union there is a network of youth clubs — places where schoolchildren can develop their talents, be they sporting, musical, artistic, or simply work-orientated. They are closely linked to the schools, and are controlled, as are the schools, by the Ministry of Education. There is no charge for the children who attend these clubs. The level of pay for the teachers is extremely low – much lower than the average wage level in the country. Therefore the standard of instruction in them is also very low.

The best teachers and best pupils tend to congregate in the central club of a town or region. This is usually called a 'Pioneers' Palace'. Thus in Leningrad there are fifteen clubs, one for each of the regions of the city, but just one Pioneers' Palace.

This whole system is the pride of the Soviet State. The idea itself is worthy of study. In my opinion, the poorer a country and its inhabitants, the greater the necessity for such a free system of children's education, in order to avoid total degradation.

And so, my friend and I, both chess players, enrolled in the chess club at the Pioneers' Palace. The director of the club was the Candidate Master Model, who had formerly been a trainer of Botvinnik. A man of broad education, with leanings towards mathematics, music and poetry, he was a splendid story-teller, and he happily shared with us numerous tales relating to chess. It is true that he gave us hardly any lectures on chess, except that he liked to show us studies. We developed independently; he split us up into groups and we began playing in tournaments. He assigned us to different catergories, depending on our initial successes.

At that time I also had other interests. I was learning to play the piano, and was a member of a literary reading (recitation) group. It is possible that I had some musical ability, but we had no piano at home, so that I had to do my practising directly in the music school. After taking lessons for a year, I gave up music, and only for a little longer did I study recitation. My 'r' sound is insufficiently pure, and I tried to remedy this defect, but without success. So I also gave up this pursuit, although for many years I retained a love for poetry, and a weakness for recitation. In the future, chess was to become my profession, and the pursuits which I had abandoned became my hobbies. I must confess that I have been unable to pass on my love for chess to my son, whereas he has inherited my interest in poetry and music to the fullest extent.

From 1944–46 I studied under the chess master Batuyev. Recently he has become better known in the world as a man who has devoted himself to the domestication of animals. Monkeys, birds and snakes live in his home, and he finds a common language with them. At the time he was working as a singer in the Academy Choir of the Leningrad Philharmonia, and was in charge of the district children's chess club. Once Batuyev noticed that I was trying to play blindfold. He sat me down with my back to the board, himself sat down, took the white pieces, and we began playing. I remember that it was a Hungarian Defence, and that I held out for about 20 moves. On the conclusion of the game, Batuyev said: 'Good lad, you'll become a master!' Ten years later we were to return (and will return with the reader) to this conversation.

When the war ended, V. G. Zak, who had been a teacher at the Pioneers' Palace before the war, returned from the army. He took charge of chess work in the Palace, and I, as one of the best players there, began studying directly with him. From 1945–48 Zak was the only teacher in the Palace chess club. Now, for comparison, there are five. Since there were so many lads, there was no chance of Zak lecturing. But sometimes I would play friendly games against him, and at other times he would show me his analysis. Zak invited masters and grandmasters to come and help. There were masters playing in the city youth championship. Thus in 1946 I first met the master Furman at the board. Grandmasters Levenfish and Bondarevsky used to give lectures. This was all most instructive.

Zak had a knack of recognizing an ability for chess in a child who had just been brought to the Palace by his mother, and who at that moment hardly knew how to move the pieces. He had many pupils, a number of them really talented. Thus Zak spotted the talent of Spassky, managed to interest him still further in chess, and arranged it so that Spassky and his family were given material support; in other words, from the age of ten Spassky was included on the pay-roll of the State, like any major athlete.

Many years later, when the pupils of our teacher gathered to celebrate his sixtieth birthday, I made a speech, and remarked that many of his characteristics had been passed on to us, his pupils. Scrupulously honest, a man of principles, and devoted to his favourite art, by his attitude to work he instilled in us and in his fellow-teachers a model, aristocratically truthful attitude to life. Others may be able to tell better, but I would like to think that I personally acquired a great deal from him. I am proud of these attributes, and I am very grateful to Zak for having cultivated them in me.

Zak also kept an eye on the competitive spirit of his pupils. I re-call how, in a qualifying tournament for the USSR Youth Championship, I lost a game, and wrote him a tearful letter, full of self-reproach. I received an immediate and cheering reply, in which Zak reassured me, and showed that there was no need for me to lose heart. And after this I did indeed cheer up and, to Zak's delight, proved that I was the strongest player in the tournament.

I made my way up the grades fairly rapidly, and by early 1946 had already reached first category rating. But my progress was tortuous, and included occasional serious set-backs. It has been said that I have good competitive endurance. But a sportsman acquires such endurance only by the difficulties which he has to overcome. And if there are no difficulties, if everything is easy, then at some point, when a testing moment nevertheless arrives, it will be more difficult for such a person to endure it, than for one who is battle-hardened. This, incidentally, is what happened with Spassky. At first he was favoured by fortune, but then came a time when adversity struck him. He turned out to be helpless, and several years of his life went by before he was able to temper his character in battle.

My first serious set-back was in the 1946 Leningrad Youth Championship. At the start I lost three games in a row. I suffered a great deal, became bad tempered, almost cried. Then I won my five remaining games, but even so did not take first place. It would not be out of place to recall another such set-back. In the semi-final of the 1950 USSR Championship I lost six games in a row and in the first nine rounds I scored just one point! I battled on, and while my victorious opponents complimented me on my creativity and spirit the points just would not come! At the finish I gained something of a revenge for my misfortunes, scoring five out of six. This tournament also did much to make me 'battle-hardened'.

But let's return to my earlier years. One of my testing grounds was the Youth Championship of the Country. In 1946, when I first took part in this tournament, I scored 5 points out of 15, while the winner, with the splendid result of 14 out of 15, was Candidate Master Tigran Petrosian. In 1947, in the same tournament, I played much more confidently, and battled it out for first place with I. Nei. In the last round I managed to scrape a draw against my main rival, to win the tournament without losing a single game with a score of $11\frac{1}{2}$ out of 15.

In 1948 the Individual Youth Championship was again held, only this time there were qualifying semi-finals tournaments. It was at the start of the semi-final that things misfired, which led to my writing the letter to Zak. I reached the final, and there, by scoring 4 out of 6, I shared first place with Nei, losing to him in our individual encounter.

A Youth Team Tournament of the Country was held in 1949. The Leningrad team won all its matches, and took first place without difficulty. This wasn't surprising: the team included (with their present-day titles) grandmasters Korchnoi, Spassky and Lutikov! On top board I scored $5\frac{1}{2}$ out of 6, and for this success was awarded the title of Candidate Master.

At the same time, I also made an effort to take part in adult events, in particular the qualifying tournaments for the Leningrad Championship. In 1948 I participated in such a tournament without particular success, failing to reach 50%, but I managed to qualify for the city championship final tournament held early in 1950. Here I excelled myself: in my games against the five masters who were competing, I scored $4\frac{1}{2}$ points. I easily won as Black in 27 moves against my main rival, Taimanov (game 1), who was, by five years, my elder. In the end I nevertheless finished half a point behind him, and took second place. Even so, this was my first major success, my first success in an adult tournament.

* 3 *

University–The Master Title

It is habitually said that chess players have a leaning towards the exact sciences, and one agrees. In my life I have often come into contact with people who work in exact professions, in particular mathematicians, and they have always shown an interest in chess. Many have themselves been chess players, sometimes rather weak, but never showing a complete lack of talent – the laws of logic prevent them from making really bad moves. Among the ranks of famous chess names there are a number of representatives of the sciences, such as Lasker, Euwe and Botvinnik.

On the other hand, we observe among chess players a number of representatives of the arts – Alekhine, Tal, and others. Evidently chess players of high class must possess a versatile brain, where logical thinking is combined with creative imagination. But the exact sciences demand an exact approach and require time for them to be seriously and correctly assimilated, whereas the arts are not so demanding. It is sufficient to know the principles in general, but not necessarily specific, terms.

For myself, I completed my schooling – ten years of it – in 1948. I was all right at mathematics, but bad at physics. I realized that logic alone was not enough in order to master physics; there was material to be studied; by then I already had no time to spare outside of chess.

There could be no question at that time of playing chess professionally. More, accurately, chess could not be called a profession. One had to complete a course at an Institute. I knew that Smyslov was a student at an Institute of Aviation, that Geller was a specialist in political economics, and that Averbakh was a chemist.

Now I had to chose a higher education establishment for my further education. I rejected the sciences as demanding too much labour. I considered the arts, and finally chose history. From childhood I had loved historical stories, and had read books on history. Like the majority of young people in the country, who in choosing for themselves a vocation had little idea of what they would be studying, I too, in choosing history, had no idea that in Stalin's time this was a rubbishy subject, which did not even deserve the high title of 'science',* and where red was readily passed off as blue, and white as black.

Within the walls of Leningrad University I spent six years. All this time, instead of studying history, I was given an extended course in Marxism. I had one friend, an excellent student, who after the second year, realizing how pointless the course was, left, having lost two years of his life. He went on to a mining institute. This was a demonstration of will-power and intelligence – to have the ability at the appropriate moment to cut off from yourself a part, so that the body continues to live a full life. I did not have the strength of mind to follow his example. The waste of two years seemed to me to be an irreparable loss. Decades were to pass before I realized that, in studying history, I had lost a great deal more. I should have entered a modern languages course. To a chess player, whatever his political views, languages are essential.

It is with disgust that I recall my years spent at university. I have a memory of meetings and conferences dedicated to the 70th Anniversary of Comrade Stalin's birth, Young Communist League meetings – tedious, distasteful, enlivened only rarely by so-called 'personal matters', i.e. the 'slating' of certain students. Interference in private life, interference in the very thoughts of the students – this was normal. I was an indifferent student. What I found especially difficult were the so-called social-economic disciplines – dialectical materialism and political economics, evidently due to the insufficient degree of logic within these sciences, and the absence of a logical connection between them and life itself. In the state exam taken on concluding the course at the Institute, I received a 'three'†️ in these subjects. But things were worse during the actual course. For a three in an exam taken during term time, a student was deprived of his stipend for the next six months. The question of whether the exam could be retaken so as to obtain a good mark, and

---

* In the Soviet Union, the literal name for the Arts is 'Humanitarian Sciences' (Translator).
† Marks awarded in exams go from one to five, anything less than a four evidently being considered unsatisfactory (Translator).

therefore a stipend, was decided by special Komsomol Organ-izations. Thus on receiving a three in my second year, I went along to the second year Komsomol office, to my fellow-students, who said to me: 'What do you want to resit for, after all, you're a chess player!' They said that only a real student required a stipend, whereas there was no reason why I should be studying, let alone receiving a stipend. ('And perhaps they were right', I now think to myself.) So I came out with nothing, but remembered for my whole life this lesson on the peculiarities of comradely relationships in the Soviet Union.

I finished at the Institute in 1954, after a delay of a year in the handing over of my diploma. Today, twenty-three years later, I am unable to remember either the content, or even the title of my diploma work. I think that it was called something like 'The Popular Front and the Communist Party in France on the eve of the Second World War'.

While at university, I studied chess intensively. I spent much time working at home, analysing grandmaster games and annotating my own. I also played a great deal – up to 90 games in a year. I took part in qualifying tournaments for the USSR championship, in the Leningrad championship, in championships of the student society 'Nauka', in student team events inside the university, and sometimes I played *hors concours* in certain tournaments by invitation.

Early in 1951 a massive Chigorin Memorial Tournament was held in Leningrad. I won a number of quite good games, but on the whole I was not happy with my play. In addition, I reached the master norm, though not altogether honestly. The point was that in the last round I needed to win, but I was up against an experienced master. Our game was adjourned in a dead drawn position. But being a young player, I had a number of supporters, including some of the organizers of the tournament. They put strong pressure on my opponent, threatening not to hand over the cash prize due to him, if he did not agree to their demands. In the end my opponent succumbed to this blackmail, and he found a way to lose the drawn position. I must admit that throughout this unsavoury episode I behaved quite improperly. I made out that I knew nothing of what was happening, and laughed at my opponent. I now wish that I had had the determination to decline the services of my supporters, and to cut short this 'charade'.

I wasn't given the master title then. At that time the All-Union Rating Committee checked on the quality of games played by each contender for the higher title. And, no doubt, this game influenced the thinking of the Committee members. But for my success in the tournament I was admitted to a semi-final tournament of the next USSR Championship, which, incidentally, I had not been able to reach from the quarter-final.

In this semi-final I at last achieved the master norm without any assistance. I recall that this wasn't easy. Towards the finish I had to win virtually all my games, and indeed I did win three games in a row. On the final day all I needed to gain the master norm was a draw, but if I won then I would go forward into the 19th USSR Championship final tournament. A tempting alternative!

But I had to play against Smyslov, already at that time the number two chess player in the world. He had gone through the tournament with ease, and was already assured of first place. As I was later told, Smyslov was not disposed towards playing that evening. Anticipating a quick draw, he had bought tickets for the theatre, and his wife was waiting for him. But that's not what happened!

I was eager for a fight – but only managed to spoil Smyslov's evening. After five hours' play our game was adjourned in an unclear position. During the night I analysed it together with Tolush. On resumption, I, with difficulty, succeeded in saving the game (game 2).

Talking of Tolush, I cannot avoid mentioning one further episode. Once, early in 1950, the director of the Leningrad Chess Club informed me that one of the best masters in the country, Tolush, had offered me his assistance as a trainer. 'I'll make a master out of him in two years', said Tolush. 'I'll manage without him', I replied to the director. I did indeed become a master, but later on I had time to reflect on what I had rejected. Spassky began working with Tolush, and within a few years everyone was surprised at how his tactical ability had developed. Tolush was a splendid master of attack, and he regenerated his talent and raised it to great heights in Spassky. It is said that when Spassky was playing in a training tournament in 1953, one of his first events under the direction of Tolush, the latter ordered Spassky not to come to see him if he had not sacrificed something in his game the day before. Spassky has rejected this tale as being untrue, but I believe it. Such 'personal violence' was quite in the spirit of Tolush, and had a beneficial influence on the development of Spassky's chess talent. I consider that my tactical ability was not inferior to that of the best attacking players, but on my own I did not succeed in developing it to the extent that I would have liked. Tactical flair, and the ability to sacrifice material for the initiative are qualities which I admire greatly in games by the masters of attack, in particular Spassky.

And so, I became one of the fifty chess masters in the country, and received my Master of Sport badge, no. 3901. It is interesting to note that twenty-five years later there are about forty grandmasters and over 500 masters in the USSR. If it is conceded that among them there were people who played quite good chess, it is obvious that there has been a reckless inflation of both these titles.

At that time I was a frail young man, and did not give the appearance of being an athlete, although I wore on my lapel my 'Master of Sport' badge. Once the Leningrad player Noakh said to me: 'Chess requires a great deal of physical and nervous energy. You have to be strong to play well. I advise you to eat oatmeal porridge every morning.' And I began to do so. This was very convenient for my stepmother, who would cook my food for the whole day, then go out to work until evening. She would often cook me a pan of porridge – for the whole day. This was hardly a varied diet, but on the other hand it was nourishing. I became accustomed to eating porridge, and over the years I have put on weight, and, evidently, improved my physical constitution.

Unfortunately, I do not possess the thoroughness of those who try not to lose anything that they have produced or mastered, and who write down their games on two scoresheets, so as to keep a record of them, and to use them for subsequent self-improvement. The majority of my games of that period remain unpublished. I then played quite differently from the way I do now – more sharply than Browne or Ljubojević. I hope that the few games which have been accidentally preserved will give some idea of my style at that time.

4

First Encounters at High Level

In 1952, to the surprise of many, including myself, I succeeded in qualifying from the USSR championship semi-final in Minsk, to the final. Much has been written about how lucky young players are. This surprising phenomenon causes bewilderment among older players, and delights the fans. That's what happended in Minsk. In this high-class tournament I saved or won a series of hopeless positions and ended up sharing second place. Behind me were Flohr, Averbakh, Holmov, and several other strong players.

In preparing for the tournament, I had been forced to give some thought to my opening repertoire. At that time I played only 1 e4 as White; as Black I played the Sicilian, and replied to 1 d4 with 1 . . . f5, choosing various forms of the Dutch. Theory was then relatively undeveloped, and there was no *Informator*, but, even so, the number of good players was quite considerable, so that I would occasionally come a cropper.

I was justified in considering my opening repertoire to be unsuitable. For the championship I began preparing a new opening – the Grünfeld Defence. From the literature available to me, I copied out about a hundred Grünfelds, and analysed them. I gained the feeling that in any variation of the Grünfeld I could obtain the advantage with Black. (An interesting thought was once expressed by Bondarevsky: 'When a player decides to change his openings, it's a sign that he's growing up!').

The Grünfeld Defence became a reliable weapon for me and, since 1952, it has served me well over the years. In my turn I have done much to ensure that this opening has become an indispensable part of any tournament. I have succeeded in introducing many new ideas, and enlivening it, after it had at one time fallen into disfavour.

The USSR Championship is a stern test for any newcomer. The

20th was a strong one, but I succeeded in taking sixth place – ahead of Smyslov, Bronstein, Keres, Suetin and Simagin, among others. My play was notable for its enviable tenacity, and for quite subtle endgame play. My opening play was still rather weak, but I was particularly helpless in the middle game. This deficiency of mine is noticable even now, although during the last sixteen years I have made considerable progress in this field. But if I could play straight from the opening moves into an ending, then I was capable of outplaying anyone. In particular, that is what happened in my game from the very first round. As Black I won an ending against the great Smyslov himself (game 3), and immediately showed that I was no accidental guest in the tournament.

I was involved in a number of games in that championship that I remember very well. Take the game with Bronstein, for instance. Up till then I had always played 1 e4 and, in the event of 1 . . . e5, the Italian Game or the Evans Gambit. Against him, out of timidity, I played solid 4 d3. We played six moves according to the book 4 d3 Nf6 5 Nc3 d6 6 Bg5, but then Bronstein played something new to me (6 . . . Na5), and I sensed that White (!) was faced with serious difficulties. I lost this game, and from then on gave up playing tne Italian Game and gradually gave up 1 e4 altogether.

A few rounds later I played the World Champion Botvinnik (game 4). I opened 1 c4. A closed position was reached, in which move by move Botvinnik began to outplay me. Several of his moves I guessed, others I did not, but the ideas behind his moves were quite incomprehensible to me. Some six to eight years were to pass before I was able to assimilate this lesson in positional play given to me by Botvinnik. I was outplayed by all the rules (although at that time I did not know such rules); then I ran short of time. But Botvinnik began to get nervous. He could have won the exchange (30 . . . Ne3), but, fearing something or other, passed over this winning possibility, then another (34 . . . B×e4) – and the game was adjourned in a position where many considered that I had the better chances. I analysed the position quite well, found some adequate counterplay for Botvinnik, and we agreed to a draw without resuming. I showed Botvinnik my analysis, and he complimented me on its quality.

The game with Keres also sticks in my memory. On encountering a young player for the first time, Keres would approach such a game with a great sense of responsibility. And that's how it was in our game. Keres exploited my inaccurate play, by a pawn sacrifice gained a strong initiative, and won as early as the 22nd move. Henceforth I regarded Keres with deference, even fear. He became for ever my most difficult opponent. I was not only unable to outplay him, I could not even obtain the better position against him. Here is an interesting psychological detail: some twenty or more years later, in what was for me a very difficult situation, on the eve of my match with Karpov, Keres was one of the few grandmasters who offered me his help. I was forced to decline, so overwhelming was his authority over me.

During the first half of the tournament, when I was one of the leaders, the veteran master Kan said to me approvingly: 'Ah, you're in second place!' 'I'll be first yet!' was my reply to him. Kan chuckled. 'Modesty is a virtue' was how he concluded. I had nothing to learn regarding self-confidence! In an article after the tournament, Kan wrote about the talent of the young players, and about me in particular. He remarked both on my poor physical preparation, and on my serious time scrambles.

It was early days yet, but after my success in this championship I felt that I could win against anyone I pleased. But things worked out quite the opposite. I saw a great deal during that championship, and received many lessons, but assimilated little. And it took a lot out of me. During the next six months my play was uneven. True, in the 1953 Leningrad Championship I again took second place, this time behind Furman. And in the summer I displayed quite a high standard in the championship of the student society 'Nauka', scoring 14 out of 16.

It was during that same summer, in a team event, that I first played against Tal. It is a psychological mystery of chess that players of the same class can have similar results in tournaments, but in games between themselves one regularly outplays the other. Ten years ago I drew up the following circle: Tal beats Portisch, Portisch beats Keres, Keres beats me, I beat Tal, Tal beats Portisch etc. Indeed, my score against Tal is 13–2 with roughly 25 draws. What is the reason? Why was it that Tal, even in his best years, when he was moving towards the world championship defeating everyone in turn in the most inconceivable style, was unable to play against me? As in the case of me against Keres, I must look for an explanation in the very first game between us. So, I was already an experienced master, and he a mere candidate master; I was twenty-two-years-old, he was sixteen, I was a pawn up, he, naturally, was a pawn down, and he offered me a draw! True, there were opposite-coloured bishops on the board, but there were also other, heavy pieces. Evidently the self-confidence of this lad surpassed even my own! It wasn't easy to win, but on the 94th move I nevertheless overcame him – in this game, and, so it would seen, for ever. From this time on he would play against me as if doomed. I can boast that Tal even played the exchange variation against my French Defence! And what's more, in our games the colours were of no great importance – as White, Tal proved even more vulnerable.

Professionalism: Towards the Grandmaster Title

In the life of a young chess player, a difficult moment arises when he finishes his higher education. He has to decide whether he is happy working in his specialized field, or whether he should devote himself entirely to what has until recently been his favourite hobby. I was fortunate. Towards the end of my university course I achieved a series of important chess successes and attracted the attention of the heads of the USSR Sports Committee, and of the Chess Federation; I was enrolled on the staff of the professional athletes of the country – 'on a stipend', as they say in the Soviet Union.

It is difficult to imagine a chess amateur – a man who works at a factory or in a school or institute, and who every year goes off to play in tournaments for three to four months, or even half a year. Who wants such a worker? Unlike many other international federations, FIDE (the International Chess Federation) does not draw any distinction between professionals and amateurs.

Regarding the material basis of chess professionalism, it was only in the USSR, from the first post-war years, that the system was introduced of the supporting of athletes by the State, enabling an athlete to use his time freely for self-improvement in his favourite pursuit. The system is unusual. The rates of pay were established in about 1949. At one time it was good money, but inflation has had its effect. The rates have been reviewed by the Ministry of Finance, but the upper limit remains unchanged. It is curious that the size of the stipend depends upon the degree of success of the athlete, and if a man no longer produces good results, he is regarded as having no prospects, and his stipend is withdrawn altogether. Of course, during the years that he is pursuing his sport he is disqualified from having another profession, the more so since the holding of more than one job is in principle forbidden (Botvinnik, who combined his grandmaster's stipend with his pay as a specialist electrical engineer was a rare exception), and so his higher education no longer counts for anything.

The fixing and withdrawing of stipends is carried out by secret departments of the sports organizations; officially there is no professionalism! The athletes arrive once a month, sign the pay-roll, leave their trade union and Party dues, and then disappear for a whole month.

An athlete's pay varies from 60 to 300 roubles a month. The average wage in the country is about 150 roubles a month. According to the official exchange rate, $1 = 75 kopecks, i.e. 300 roubles is equivalent to $400. But on the black market you can get at least five roubles for a dollar, and the Soviet State assesses its currency at roughly the same rate. For citizens who earn abroad, and wish to buy goods in the Soviet Union for convertible foreign currency, the State issues special securities – 'certificates' – which can be exchanged for goods in special shops where the prices are many times lower than in shops for the average citizen.

As you can see, athletes don't receive big money. For all the 'State professionalism' of Soviet athletes, they nevertheless remain amateurs on the money that they receive. But, even so, the success of Soviet chess players can be explained chiefly in terms of State support, and the introduction of 'stipends' for chess players has played a virtually decisive role in their development.

At the start of 1954 I once again played in the USSR Championship (the 21st). I played well, scored a number of impressive wins, and was an active contender for first place. But I couldn't keep it up for the whole tournament. Towards the finish I lost a couple of games to second rank players.* Averbakh overtook me, and I shared second place with Taimanov. For the first time I came up against Petrosian in the All-Union arena. We had met once before in a schoolboy tournament, when he had been invincible. Here I came ahead of him. It was from this point that my rivalry with Petrosian began, a rivalry which was soon to turn into war.

After this championship, I played for the first time in my life in an international tournament – in Bucharest. The tournament was

---

* This is hardly correct: Korchnoi lost in round fourteen (out of nineteen) to Bannit, who finished equal fourteenth (out of twenty), and in round seventeen to Lisitsin, who finished equal fourth (Translator).

made up mainly of masters, but at that time there where few grandmasters in the world. The masters were strong – Furman, Nezhmetdinov, Holmov, Pachman. The battle for first place resolved itself into a race between Nezhmetdinov and myself. A talented master of attack, Nezhmetdinov normally played unevenly, but in this tournament was at his best. In the first round I miraculously managed to draw against him the exchange and a pawn down (game 5). Following this, the two of us stormed ahead, and before the last round we were leading the tournament, with $12\frac{1}{2}$ each out of 16. On the last day I had an uneventful draw with O'Kelly, while Nezhmetdinov lost to Furman. Thus I won the tournament.

Then came the 1954 World Students' Team Championship at Oslo. By present-day standards the Soviet student team was very weak – we had playing for us only two semi-grandmasters – Moiseyev and me – and the remainder were masters. We naturally found it difficult against certain teams, who were represented by what was virtually their full national side. Thus we only just saved the match against Bulgaria – here I lost to Minev – and we lost to the Czechs, who, led by Filip, came out a point ahead of us, $1\frac{1}{2}$–$2\frac{1}{2}$. The following year I played badly in the USSR Championship, so that I was not picked for the student team. Instead, it was decided to strengthen the team by including one of the prize-winners from the championship, Spassky, and also Taimanov, who had long ceased to be a student, but who on the other hand was one of the strongest players in the country at that time. Thus in 1955 at Lyons the Soviet student team had no difficulties.

However, the student team in 1956, at Uppsala, turned out to be even stronger. Just imagine: myself, almost a grandmaster, semi-grandmasters Tal and Polugayevsky, and masters Lutikov, Vasyukov and Antoshin. Most of the students came to enjoy themselves, to drink wine, and to stay up late, but we played seriously, and there was no question of any disturbance of our routine. It was not surprising that we defeated the Yugoslav team, which included two grandmasters, by a clean score. I won as Black against Matanović (game 6), while Tal won a now well-known game against Ivkov. The Yugoslavs were our main rivals; after this encounter the way became clear.

The tournament concluded with a simultaneous display tour through Sweden and Norway. By present-day standards the rates were paltry. I remember that we gave a display in a certain Swedish club. Kotev (the leader of our delegation) received 150 Krona, I received 100, and Tal 50. The future World Champion gave a simultaneous display for $10!

After this I took part in no further student events. At present, the selection of the USSR student team is taken just as seriously as it was then. There must definitely be at least two or three grandmasters in the team . . .

The 22nd USSR Championship in 1955 was a zonal or qualifying tournament for the world championship. All the best players naturally took part, even the world champion, Botvinnik, who competed *hors concours*. Success was expected of me, since I had distinguished myself in the previous years, but I did not live up to expectations. I cannot complain of being unlucky; I managed to save a game against Keres when the exchange down, and against Averbakh, when a pawn down. I fought in every game, but without success. My first win (which was also the last) came in the thirteenth round. I racked my brains, trying to discover the cause of my lack of success: I was criticized severely, accused of being conceited, of not keeping to a regular routine, and of being drunk. These latter accusations were not altogether unjustified, although in one's youth the strict adherence to a routine does not play such an important role as it does in later years.

An article appeared in the chess press, written by Bronstein – the only outstanding player who was an onlooker at the 22nd Championship. His sympathetic criticism is worth quoting: '. . .The people of Leningrad must help one of the most talented of Soviet chess players, Viktor Korchnoi, to overcome the crisis he is experiencing. Already in the twenty-first championship . . . he showed signs of underrating his opponents, and of a desire to win any position, by any means, without there being sufficient objective preconditions. Here, in stronger company, after a few reversals he lost faith in himself, but for this there is no justification.' My thanks to Bronstein, who was the only one to support me at that time. I suffered a great deal.

For the first time in my life, with the aim of raising the standard of my play, I gave up smoking. For the first time, I went for medical treatment, to a sanitorium in Sochi. And I also applied myself to improving my theoretical knowledge. Two months later I was Champion of Leningrad, where I established one of my first records:

I scored 17 points out of 19 games. Three points behind was the second prize-winner, Tolush, and a further two behind in third place was Furman. After four rounds I had $2\frac{1}{2}$ points, but then I won eleven games in a row! The Leningrad chess school has always been thought to be pretty strong. It is no accident that, in the matches over 40 boards between Moscow and Leningrad, the Leningrad players, although inferior on paper, have always fought persistently, and have won more frequently than their more distinguished opponents. Thus the winning of the Leningrad Championship with such a result immediately placed me among the strongest players in the country. I was included in the USSR team which took part in the European Team Championship, and at the end of the year was sent to the tournament in Hastings.

It is unlikely that the Western reader will be able to appreciate the significance for a Soviet citizen of being able to travel abroad.

The iron curtain is no figment of the imagination. The Soviet authorities are not interested in showing to their people the Western World, but try to maintain the impression that the USSR is the only country in the world which is fit to live in. For the Soviet man who wishes to see the world, all sorts of barriers are erected in his path. There are questionnaires, containing questions of every kind, designed to establish how loyal the citizen is, questionnaires which, in many instances, will later be checked. There are Party meetings, irrespective of whether he is a Party member, and Committees – first Regional, then Municipal, then All-Union – which, one after another, must grant permisssion to leave. For the ordinary person there is also a monetary duty – in the form of the high cost of the journey, or the high price payable for a foreign passport. There is also personal surveillance of a Soviet citizen while he is travelling and while he is in the foreign country – with the aim that he should become more familiar with historical monuments than with the everyday life of the country. It should be added that very little money is given to the average Soviet man (and to take out Soviet roubles and change them at any exchange rate is strictly forbidden), so that, however much he economizes, he will not feel inclined to go out into such splendid places as Selfridges, Samariten, or Beinkorf.

A man going abroad on official business has significant advantages over the ordinary citizen. The selection procedure and the checking are somewhat relaxed – after all, he is an expert, who normally has already seen something of the world. The system, however, remains the same and document regristration takes considerably longer than a month. Personal surveillance is reduced, the monetary duty is lowered, and additional money is provided for the person's stay in the foreign country. This last circumstance plays an important role, especially since an expert may be able to count on receiving prizes or fees in the country he is going to. In view of the low level of pay in the USSR, the impossibility of purchasing high-quality goods, and the inadequate exchange of goods with the West, every visit to the West is a great help financially, and the visitor can purchase articles which distinguish him from his grey surroundings.

A trip abroad is thus an event of exceptional importance and value. If a major specialist, who has been nominated for a visit to a foreign country, suddenly stays at home, there is no good reason except that his trip has been cancelled. This means that he has become a person who is forbidden to travel. The reasons for this are of course not given, but sooner or later they will come to light. It may be the existence of a relative abroad (thus Holmov has never played in tournaments in capitalist countries), 'immoral' behaviour, such as frequent marital changes (e.g. Tal between 1968 and 1972), incautious political pronouncements (Spassky, after his match with Fischer), reprimands for bad conduct abroad (Korchnoi, 1962–65). However, I seem to be jumping ahead. . . .

We played a preliminary qualifying round of the European Team Championship against Poland at Lodz in 1955. I recall one particular episode that was rather unpleasant for me. It was clear that we were going to win the match by a big score, something like 17–3. On the first day I won as White against Doda, but in the second round, playing the master Branicki, I failed to gain an advantage. We both ran short of time, and then our flags fell simultaneously. It wasn't clear how many moves had been made, for we had repeated the position several times. If it had been repeated four times, then the game was a draw, if only three times, then White had lost on time. The leader of our delegation, Abramov, a fairly tactful person, suggested that I should agree to a draw but, in the heat of battle, I was stubborn. As a young man I hardly was aware of political niceties and, subconsciously, I followed the line that we were stronger not only in the chess sense, we were also a Great Power, and therefore we, which means I, had the right to decide any argument in my favour! And so I got my way, and was awarded a win. When I now recall this incident, I feel ashamed. Incidentally, nineteen years later Tal was to protest strongly, again in a debatable situation, when, having already resigned a game, he got a control committee to count the moves played and establish that his opponent had a prior loss on time. This also took place in Poland against a Polish chess player.

Three of us set off in December 1955 for the New Year tournament in Hastings. Taimanov and I had a supervisor attached to us, someone by the name of Zaitsev, whose main function was to keep an eye on us. True, things could have been worse: subsequently Zaitsev was to become one of the diplomatic staff in the USA, and, playing in the State of Virginia, even reached the American Master norm.

The tournament proceeded without any great difficulties for me. I won a couple of good games, including one against Ivkov, who was then already a famous grandmaster. In the decisive game against my chief rival Olafsson, I played a draw as Black, and as a result shared first place with him. Taimanov finished in fourth place, outside the prize list. It is interesting to note how modest the prizes were then. In a tournament of ten players there were three prizes, of £60, £40 and £20! I recall also an episode from my game with Taimanov (game 7). He was rather afraid of me and, since I had White, he persuaded me to 'compose' the game. It turned out to be quite brilliant. Later, in his book *Chess Encounters*, he went into raptures about how brilliantly we had played – but in fact the whole game had been worked out beforehand!

Straightaway after Hastings I took part in the 23rd USSR Championship. I played listlessly, with many draws. I recall playing a difficult ending against Tolush, where I had two knights which had to fight against a rook and two enemy passed pawns on opposite wings. After unbelievable efforts I succeeded in stopping these pawns and securing a draw (game 8). In the foyer, I ran into my old teacher Batuyev. 'How well you played that' he said, 'You'll be a grandmaster!'

By the finish I managed to pull myself together, scoring four from my last five games. In the penultimate round I defeated Spassky (game 9), who was already then one of the World Championship Candidates. Against the King's Indian, I adopted a comparatively new method of play 5 b3, which was later to become popular at master level, and without much difficulty obtained an overwhelming advantage. Incidentally, when playing against

Spassky I inevitably experienced difficulty if I met him in the first half of a tournament, but if the draw brought us together in the second half (more often than not in the penultimate round), things were difficult for him. Putting great efforts into every game, Spassky was clearly lacking in strength at the end of a protracted event.

I took fourth place, half a point behind Taimanov, Averbakh and Spassky, who shared first place. According to the rules then in force, the USSR grandmaster title was awarded to a player who twice finished third within the space of three years. Apart from my second-third place in 1954, and my fourth place here, there were also my victories in Bucharest and Hastings, and on the sum total of these successes I was awarded the Grandmaster title. My ticket was number 18. At the FIDE Congress at the end of the year, I was also awarded the International Grandmaster title.

* 6 *

Life as a Grandmaster

Next came the Student Olympiad in Uppsala, and the tour of Sweden and Norway already mentioned. Then I moved on directly to Central Asia, to the town of Frunze, where, *hors concours*, I took part in a USSR Championship quarter-final tournament.

It is not that easy to leave Western Europe and travel to the depths of Asia on the same day – the difference in living conditions is flabbergasting. But I didn't play too badly. In this little-known tournament I scored 18 out of 19, my only loss being in the 18th round.

In the summer, Soviet players visited Yugoslavia for the first time. This was one of the first contacts with a country which, though situated in Eastern Europe, had allowed itself to pursue an independent political line. We arrived there before the diplomats did – they still had to establish official relations. The Yugoslav players were seeing us for the first time, and they could not yet have guessed what a formidable force we – Soviet professionals – were! I remember how at the airport I was interviewed and asked who was the strongest player among us. I named myself! What else can a young man say? In fact even then the Yugoslavs had an excellent theoretical grounding, and it was not easy playing against them. I was crushed by Djurašević, but won two dubious games; one of them, it is true, was against that solid player Trifunović, the other – a game abounding in mistakes – was against Milić.

From Yugoslavia to the Ukraine, where the 'Burevestnik' tournament was held in Poltavo. Here I shared first place with the master Kotkov with 12 points out of 16. According to the rules, I had to play a match of six games with him, and this took place in his home town of Permi-Molotov. In principle I am against the division of players into tournament players and match players, as has been suggested by Bronstein. There are strong players and weak ones, anything else is a contrivance. And in my first match I demonstrated this. It lasted only four games, and I won by the score of $3\frac{1}{2}-\frac{1}{2}$.

1957 was the year of Tal's brilliant rise to fame. Earlier, in the semi-final tournament of the 24th Soviet championship in Tbilisi, he had only just made the prize list (not surprising in such company as Petrosian, Polugayevsky, Korchnoi, Krogius and other distinguished names), and then in the final events he began with four straight wins. I recall my game with him from the fifth round. I asked Bronstein's advice as to what I should play, and how. He replied: 'You can play what you like, but for this game you will be responsible to all the players in the tournament. You have not the right to lose it.' I was black, and the game ended in a draw (game 10). Incidentally, it was in this game that I noticed the rather stereotyped way in which Tal conducted his attack. However, Tal won this tournament, and the winner is never criticized! Eleven years later I expressed my views in the press, pointing out, against the opinion of the vast majority, the stereotyped nature of Tal's play.

In his book, *The Life and Games of Mikhail Tal*, published in 1976 by R.H.M., Tal recalls this incident, and with a certain amount of pride points out that the world champion himself, Petrosian, spoke out in defence of him. It is true that in the weekly *64* there appeared a sharp anonymous article defending Tal. It is interesting to speculate on how Tal came to know the name of the author!

In the 1957 USSR Championship final tournament I played feebly, and shared seventh place with Petrosian. But on the whole it was not a bad year for me. I played with a fair degree of success, accumulating experience for more serious battles in the future. In the Leningrad Championship I shared first place with Furman. I remember that I chose this tournament to experiment. With the aim of varying my opening repertoire, I played exclusively 1 e4. Then I played successfully in the USSR – Yugoslavia match, where I made the best individual score, thus rehabilitating myself after my failure in the previous match, and justifying to some extent my boastful announcement a year earlier.

The Yugoslavs, it must be said, were visiting the USSR for the first time. They complained that in Leningrad there were 'white nights and black days'. In fact they were quite unable to accustom themselves to the service in our country, the standard of which even to this day is much lower than that which is usual in Europe and America. Individual hospitality on the part of the hosts could not make up for this official service. The flabbergasted Yugoslavs lost this match by a crushing margin.

Following this I played for the USSR in the European Team Championship final pool in Vienna. I played on board eight, it is true, but on the other hand I scored $5\frac{1}{2}$ out of 6, achieving the best individual result. Towards the end of the year I again played in the USSR Championship semi-final – in Sverdlovsk. Here I took first place without great difficulty, winning against my main rivals – Averbakh, Gurgenidze, Simagin and Lutikov.

Naturally, I was now considered one of the favourites for the forthcoming 25th USSR Championship, which was also a qualifying tournament for the Interzonal. But it turned out badly for me. During the tournament I fell ill, and went into hospital. For the greater part of the tournament I had to play after arriving straight from the hospital to the game. In the hospital the food was bad, and there was no possibility of preparing for the next game. As a result I played very feebly. The one consolation was that I won against Tal (game 11), who once again became USSR Champion. In this tense encounter, I succeeded as black in holding Tal's onslaught. The game was already looking drawish when Tal, somewhat short of time, went in for a combination with a queen sacrifice, which met with a simple refutation.

At the beginning of 1958 there occurred an important event in my life – I got married. I met my wife-to-be in Gagra, on the Black Sea, when relaxing there in preparation for the semi-final in Sverdlovsk. My wife was born in Tbilisi, which was where all her relations were, but she was then living in Moscow, and shortly after our wedding I took her away to Leningrad. My wife loved Moscow, and several times suggested that we go back there. My friends also frequently suggested this. Why? Well. Moscow is the capital! You can live better in Moscow! But I remained faithful to the city where I had been born, and in which I had grown up. And to all attempts to persuade me, I replied that they, the advisers, had not seen Paris or New York, which were no doubt even better. So why bother changing for a trifle? Then, at that moment, I never thought then that I would be so consistent – but more about that later. . . .

The first tournament that I played in, in my new 'married' state, was in Sochi. This was the Championship of the Russian Republic. Nezhmetdinov, one of the strongest of the Soviet masters, won. For some reason he was rarely sent abroad, and so he never succeeded in becoming a grandmaster. In the tournament I shared second place with Furman and Polugayevsky, losing to the latter with White in a Sicilian. On the whole I consider the Sicilian to be a difficult opening for Black, but Polugayevsky is a genuine virtuoso in the complex play that results. In attempting to punish him for his 'dubious opening tastes', I opened 1 e4 and, like dozens of other grandmasters, was myself punished.

The 1958 USSR–Yugoslavia match played in Zagreb remains in my memory. In Zagreb, on board three, I played a match of four games with Ivkov, an opponent whom I have encountered many times during the course of two decades. I stood well in the games, but managed to score only two points. In order to level the scores I had to win the fourth and final game (game 12). I was highly dissatisfied with my result, and pleaded poor form. In fact it must be admitted that Ivkov is a very sound player, with an unusual positional sense. The twenty or so games that I have played against him have had a beneficial influence on my chess strength.

Later in the year came, as usual, the exhausting USSR Championship semi-final, where it was with difficulty that I managed to share second place with Geller (the winner was Holmov). The final tournament (the 26th) was held in Tbilisi early in 1959. I did not play particularly well, but the will of fate forced me to take part in the battle for first place.

The tournament resolved itself into a struggle for the leadership between Tal, who was then approaching the best form of his life, and Petrosian. In the penultimate round I had to play Tal (game 13), and in the last round Petrosian. The hullabaloo around the tournament was very considerable. The Georgians supported Tal, and the Armenians Petrosian. Before my game with Tal I was visited by a group of Armenians, with the request that I should deal with Tal good and proper. However, there was no need for them to have asked me. I sensed fairly keenly Tal's strengths and weaknesses, and I knew how to prepare against him. As Black in a Sicilian I fairly quickly obtained a comfortable game, and towards the adjournment won a pawn. The position was still not very easy to win, but here an interested party stepped into the act – Petrosian himself. He offered me his help in analysing the position. To me, being inexperienced in intrigues behind the scenes, such assistance seemed (and seems) not altogether respectable, but at that moment it was the game that interested me, and I of course agreed. Together we found a winning path, and on the following day I cleared the way for Petrosian to win the tournament.

But my mission in the tournament did not end with this. The Georgians began besieging me, demanding that I should now defeat Petrosian. I had White against him. But, it must be said, for years I could not adapt to Petrosian's style of play. And it is unlikely that there is anyone who can win against him 'on demand'. I made an attempt, and an interesting tactical skirmish developed. But the position soon cleared, and it became obvious that I would not be able to win. 'A cunning Armenian has swindled a dozen Jews' was what they said in Tbilisi, and Petrosian became Champion.

In March I took part in the Leningrad–Budapest match in Hungary. From the chess point of view the match did not prove to be particularly interesting for me. I played against Barcza, and won by the score of $2\frac{1}{2}$–$1\frac{1}{2}$. But I recall a discussion with our team captain, Bondarevsky. Just before the match the Hungarians suggested that we should play four rounds. Bondarevsky insisted on two games, and the question was discussed at a team meeting. I said that, since we were the stronger side, we should accept the conditions suggested by our opponents. It was also not difficult to understand Bondarevsky's position: reading between the lines it was implied that, since we were politically stronger, the Hungarians should accept our conditions. Despite my youth, I enjoyed considerable authority among the members of the Leningrad team, and my suggestion was accepted. The subsequent course of the match unexpectedly proved me right. On the first day our team suffered a crushing defeat; on the second day we somehow managed to gain our revenge; and only on the third and fourth days did we gain an advantage in points.

On subsequent occasions I again found myself arguing against Bondarevsky, opposing his pro-Soviet position with my own logical thinking.

* 7 *

My First Major Success

The early part of 1959 did not herald any serious qualitative improvement in my play. In the match with the Hungarians I played rather insipidly, and in the USSR Team Championship, under the patronage of the 'USSR Peoples' Spartakiad' I again did not especially distinguish myself. But in the second half of the year I was more energetic. In September I won a small tournament in Poland, at Krakow. I played even more strongly in the usual (although this was to be the last one in my life) USSR Championship Semi-Final in Chelyabinsk. I went through the tournament without a single defeat, winning a number of excellent games, and took first place without any competition. My play in the semi-final was an indisputable indication of my good form on the eve of the next Championship of the country.

The 27th final was held in Leningrad at the beginning of 1960. My living conditions were poor at the time: I lived with my wife and small child in two small rooms of a communal flat. So I asked for a room in a hotel, which is where I spent the greater part of the tournament.

I began badly with a loss to Lutikov and a draw with Taimanov. But then I began winning game after game. I could not put a foot wrong: I won every sort of game – complex and simple, from good positions and bad. If I would occasionally miscalculate in a combination, my opponent would not notice. That's what happened, for instance, in my game with Nei. In difficult positions, defending stubbornly, I saved and even won games, as happened against Shamkovich. In addition, I won a number of excellent games, of which I am proud even to this day, against Sakharov, Smyslov and Polugayevsky (games 14–16). I was progressing confidently, with my rivals – Geller and Petrosian – apparently unable to catch me. But suddenly I stumbled. Four rounds before the finish, playing against Bagirov, I picked up the wrong piece. My opponent had just taken one of my rooks, and I was considering my reply. 'First', I thought, 'I'll take his rook with my bishop, on the next move I'll move my other bishop.' The two bishops stood side by side, and I picked up the wrong one, the one that was attacking nothing. Without completing the move, I left the hall, leaving a thousand fans, who were tensely following my game, in a state of bewilderment, which shortly turned to grief. What can I say? I recall that the day was a nervy one: the baby was ill, and I had helped my wife to look after him. I recall too how, sitting on the stage, I was angry to see how two friends – Geller and Gufeld – were playing out a game which had been made up beforehand: Gufeld was quite shamelessly throwing the game. This can perhaps be explained, but certainly not forgiven.

I had three games still to play – against Krogius, Geller and Suetin. After the terrible blow I had suffered, and after a sleepless night, my mood was aggressive like never before. In a desperate struggle during which I narrowly escaped defeat, I overcame Krogius (game 17). Before my game with Geller, he was leading me by half a point. I played very sharply with black, and at one point my opponent stood better, but he was aiming only for a draw, and by exploiting his unsure play, I won (game 18). This is one of the most memorable games of my life, and it was not by accident that I annotated it for Keene's book *Learn from the Grandmasters* (Batsford). Before the last round I was now leading by half a point from Petrosian, who had white against Krogius, and Geller black against Bronstein. Soon after the start of the round I realized that I stood badly, and offered Suetin a draw (game 19). He declined, and then, before my very eyes, went and consulted with Geller and Petrosian. As was later revealed, Petrosian told him to agree to a draw, while Geller said 'Play on, you'll beat him!' In the subsequent course of the game, in a time scramble which was the more severe for me, fortune smiled on me. I won a pawn, and on resumption the game as well, thus becoming the USSR Champion for the first time in my life. Geller and Petrosian, who both won their games, finished half a point behind.

Fourteen years passed. Being on good terms with grandmaster Bronstein, I invited him to a week's training session in preparation for my match with Karpov. One day, during a friendly chat, he began reminiscing: 'Do you remember how on that February day in

1960 I "threw" my game against Geller? Why did I do it? Well, during the game I suddenly saw how unscrupulously and crudely Krogius was losing to Petrosian. I couldn't leave Petrosian as the sole winner of the championship. In an excellent position I made an incorrect piece sacrifice, and soon resigned.' 'But what about me? In that way you were betraying me as well!' I exclaimed. 'You were in a bad way, I thought you were losing, and I couldn't leave Petrosian as the sole winner', Bronstein repeated.

After reading this dialogue the reader will realize that to become Chess Champion of the USSR 'honestly' means to accomplish a great feat. However there is nothing surprising about this. In the professional chess world inside the Soviet Union, the top places lead to colossal privileges, and the battle for these places is bound to involve means not associated purely with chess. Petrosian may have realized this ahead of anyone else.

My achievement was appreciated at its true value. It lifted me into the first rank of the strongest grandmasters in the country. New chess horizons opened befor me.

It will not be out of place to mention that soon after the championship, on the initiative of the Sports Committee, I was granted a two-room flat. Up to then I had had 20 square metres in a flat where there were several families, who shared a communal kitchen, toilet and bathroom, whereas now I had 27sq.m. in a self-contained flat. In moving people from inferior flats to superior ones, the standard floor area was 9 sq.m. per person, so that my 27 sq.m. were exactly what I was entitled to. But not all families are eligible for resettlement, only those who are most needy. Thus in Leningrad the 'needy' refers to families who have less than 4 sq.m. per person. And had I not become champion, I would have had to wait a long, long time for improved conditions.

In May I played in a twelve-man international tournament in Moscow. Over the short distance I did not manage to gather sufficient momentum, and with 8 points out of 11 I took third place, half a point behind Smyslov and Holmov. In the summer I was sent to the international tournament in Buenos Aires, dedicated to the 150th Anniversary of the Argentine Republic, in which sixteen grandmasters were competing. Reshevsky played excellently, seizing the lead and outstripping his rivals by a considerable margin. Towards the finish he reduced his tempo somewhat, and I succeeded in catching him.

There, I remember, was my first encounter with Fischer. In it (game 20) he gained a slight positional advantage, and in addition my situation with regard to the clock was not altogether healthy. Perhaps he thought that I was the only one who could catch Reshevsky, who was playing so splendidly, and so he was disinclined to try to beat me [but again this was the one poor tournament of Fischer's international career and more likely form explains it – ed.]

After the tournament, several grandmasters made a tour of provincial Argentina, playing in two small tournaments. In Santa Fé, Taimanov was the winner, coming ahead of Szabó, Gligorić and myself. At the tournament in Cordoba, where there were just two grandmasters left, I finished ahead of Taimanov by half a point.

In the autumn of 1960, I first played for the Soviet team in the World Chess Olympiad. Playing on board four, I had quite good results, and I didn't lose a single game. To do this, it is true, I had to perform a minor miracle. I managed to save an adjourned game in an ending where I was a whole knight down against Borja, a player from the Philippines! However, such instances are not rare in my games. For instance, in the 1976 IBM Tournament, I managed to draw against Faragó, again a clear knight down. And in 1956, at Uppsala against Alster, I was fortunate enough to save an endgame when a bishop down. It is evidently all a question of optimism. If a player believes in miracles, he can sometimes perform them.

At the very end of the year, another interesting event took place. The 40-board matches between Moscow and Leningrad were then arranged roughly once every two years. In 1958 I had played against Bronstein. Both as white and black we had the French Defence, and with difficulty I managed to draw both games. In 1960 I met the great Botvinnik (game 21), who already at that time was making only rare appearances. On account of his venerable age [49!? – ed.], and his well-known independence of opinion, chess players were already calling him the Patriarch. I managed to beat him by 1½–½. Incidentally, the Leningrad team also won the match by one point with a score of 40½–39½. At that time Botvinnik and Tal were preparing for their return match, and my achievements in 1960 were highly valued by them. Each of them, through a third person, invited me to help in his preparations. But I remained true to myself, and declined both offers. Possibly I was wrong to do so. After all there was much I could have learned, especially from Botvinnik – by way of 'exchange of experience'. Certain players, working as trainers, have skilfully managed to enrich their knowledge for the future. But I was of the opinion that, since I myself was intending to battle for the World Championship, I shouldn't be pretending to act as a trainer.

* 8 *

For the First Time – a Candidate

At the start of 1961, the 28th USSR Championship, a qualifying tournament for the World Championship, took place. The previous year had been a pretty tense one for me, and I had not found the time to relax. This often happens with young players; they forget that chess is a difficult, exhausting game, and that, in order to conceive fresh, new ideas, a clear brain is required. That is what happened with me. After winning a couple of games at the start, I played a long series of draws, losing on the way to Smyslov and Petrosian. My chances of going through to the Interzonal appeared to be nil. But in the second half of the tournament I seemed to get my second wind. I began winning game after game, and closed right up on the leading group. My rivals were Geller, Spassky, Stein and Polugayevsky. In the penultimate round, as often happened, I defeated Spassky (game 22), and in the last round won against Polugayevsky (game 23). I thus took second place, only half a point behind the tournament winner, Petrosian. The sensation of the tournament was the success of the young master, Stein. Playing for the first time in the USSR Championship, he ended up among the prize winners. A player of enormous talent, he managed to demonstrate this in his very first appearances, as if sensing that his chess career would not be a long one.*

Of the events of 1961, the European Team Championship in Oberhausen sticks in my memory. There the USSR team easily took first place, and Smyslov and I battled it out for the best overall result. Smyslov was playing on board seven, and I on board eight, and in the end I managed to come ahead of him by half a point. I won eight games, and drew one; of the wins, I only remember the

---

* He died, aged 38, in 1973 (ed.).

one against Bilek (game 24). As was usual in our encounters, it was decided in a fearful time scramble.

There is something else that I recall from the trip to Oberhausen. On arriving back in the USSR, the deputy leader of our delegation, a man from the KGB, reported that I had behaved badly, and that I had taken the liberty of inviting a certain German lady to the cinema. Such a 'sin' had indeed occurred, although the visit to the cinema did not in fact take place. Even so, a black mark appeared in my 'personal file'.

In the autumn I played in an international tournament in Budapest. Hungarian players are noted in Europe for their class, and the tournament turned out to be a pretty strong one, especially since four Soviet players were taking part. At the start I scored $2\frac{1}{2}$ out of 3, but in round four lost to the Hungarian master Dely, and in crushing style at that. That sort of thing used to happen to me, and still does. As Black, I often stake everything on winning, which involves considerable risks. I have quite good results as black, but sometimes I am punished for my opening experiments.

It was a difficult moment in the tournament. For the first time I had white against Filip and played for a win when it was strategically unjustified. The game ended in a draw. More accurately, in a position where he stood better, Filip, being a peacable person, gave me a draw. It shows, incidentally, what tremendous talent Filip must have had, to have achieved such successes with such a mild temperament.

I then played against Bronstein. He lured me into one of his cunning opening schemes (along with his great opening erudition, he also plays the opening subtly from the psychological point of view), and I only just managed to save the draw. My next game was with Bilek (game 25). It is not often that Bilek shows himself to be a fighting player, but against me he always plays with great fervour. In a tense, sharp struggle, everything was balanced on a knife edge. This also applied literally to my flag. But it all turned out well for me in the end. I snatched an important point, and after this everything went smoothly. As a result I took first place, two points ahead of Bronstein and Filip.

In this tournament the grandmaster norm was achieved by Simagin, an interesting player, and a pleasant, witty person, who, alas, passed on from this life too soon. I won my game against him, quite convincingly (game 26). One curious point is that during the game he went up to Taimanov and said: 'Why does he look at me with such malice, as if I had slaughtered all of his family down to the sixth generation?' To be honest, competitive malice is not something that I practise. The only present-day players who could argue with me about this are Karpov, Petrosian and Fischer.

Early in 1962 the Interzonal Tournament began in Stockholm. This was perhaps the first tournament in which the young Fischer demonstrated to the world his tremendous chess strength. He overcame all his opponents with enviable ease, and three rounds before the finish had already assured himself of first place. I played quite well in the tournament, but until the last few minutes of the last round it was not clear whether or not I would qualify. My chief rival was Stein. The point was that according to the rules, not more than three Soviet players could go forward to the candidates' tournament, although the number of places available was much greater. I remembered my game with Fischer vividly (game 27). I consider that, at that time, Fischer was still a little weaker than he was to be a few years later. He gained the advantage from the opening, but then let me off the hook. In slight time trouble, I missed some drawing chances, and lost. I recall that I was very upset by this defeat. On the following day, I bet Fischer that I had stood better in the position where I had blundered. He smiled, but didn't argue.

The situation before the last day was very tense; Stein and I stood level. In the final round I had black against Yanofsky, and Stein white against Olafsson. I was worried that Yanofsky might have been prepared for our game by none other than Fischer. They were on friendly terms. I stood very badly in this game, but managed to save a sharp ending a pawn down. Stein, on the other hand, gained a menacing position against Olafsson, but then blundered and lost. As a result I shared fourth place with Filip, and went through to the Candidates'.

If I had known then all that was to happen later, I would have gladly granted Stein the dubious pleasure of playing in the Candidates' Tournament at Curaçao.

There, as we all now know, everything was arranged by Petrosian. He agreed with his friend Geller to play draws in all their games together. They also persuaded Keres to join their coalition. In a two-month long tournament, held in tropical conditions, it was important to shorten the distance by eight rounds: this gave them a great advantage over the remaining competitors. But, even so, it seems to me that Keres made a mistake. At that moment he was playing more strongly than anyone, and it was not to his advantage to take draws with his main rivals. A more crafty person, on learning about the pact between Geller and Petrosian, would have sought a separate alliance.

At first I didn't grasp what was happening in the tournament. I recall how, on seeing a ten-move draw between Geller and Petrosian in the second cycle, I asked Geller whom he was intending to beat. 'You!' was his direct reply. I merely shrugged my shoulders. At that point I was playing better than Geller, was superior to him generally, and had no intention of losing to him.

Meanwhile, fatigue was stealing up on the more simple-minded participants in the tournament. Filip began playing more and more weakly with every round, while after the third cycle, owing to extreme tiredness, Tal fell ill with kidney trouble, and had to leave the tournament. After the first cycle, I was in the lead. Fatigue began to tell on me as early as the second cycle. In a position where I had a big advantage, I blundered away a piece to Fischer. A week's rest in unfamiliar tropical conditions on the Island of Saint Maarten did nothing to ease the situation. In the next cycle I lost in turn to each of the three leaders. It was this that persuaded Fischer to write after the tournament that I had been chosen 'as a sacrifice' by the Soviet delegation. Surely he wasn't being serious. I am incapable, by character, of being made a sacrifice, the more so since, if I had won those three games, it wouldn't have been Petrosian who would have won the tournament!

And so, Petrosian was the winner, finishing ahead of Geller and Keres by half a point. The decisive game in the battle between Keres and Petrosian proved to be the Benko–Keres encounter from the fourth and final cycle. It was adjourned in a position where Benko had a slight advantage. Up till this time Keres had won all the games that he had played against Benko – four in the 1959 Candidates' in Yugoslavia, and three at Curaçao. The same would probably have happened here, had not Petrosian interfered. On the initiative of Petrosian's wife, a painstaking night of analysis was arranged. From whatever point of view – ethical or political – this would seem to be monstrous. But the deed was done: Benko won the game, and Petrosian the tournament. Later, Petrosian's wife proudly explained in Moscow how she had made her husband

World Champion. True, there was still the match with Botvinnik to come, but he was now over fifty years old. In the first half of the match, Petrosian exhausted Botvinnik with draws, and in the second half easily exploited his advantage in age.

We should not belittle Petrosian's talent and merits. Lower class by birth, he became acquainted with the noble game, mastered it to perfection, and even left his mark. The 'Petrosian style' became a well-used term. For years, chess masters regarded his inimitable style with contempt and fear. With the elevation of Petrosian to the chess throne, thousands of chess amateurs were forced to reconsider their views on the attractiveness and nobleness of the game.

On losing the match in 1963, Botvinnik expressed the opinion that Petrosian was a rare exception in chess, in that he was not a creator, but a destroyer of values in the process of creation. This is true. It remains for me to add that this not only applies to chess. One cannot help but admire the devilish determination and ingenuity of this man.

* 9 *

First Difficulties and
First Illness

The Soviet delegation at Curaçao included a man who had nothing
to do with chess. He was a colonel 'in civvies', as a prominent
member of the KGB is usually called. On our return to the USSR,
he wrote a report in which he pointed out my improper behaviour at
Curaçao. The chief sin noted by him was that I had permitted
myself to have a go at the casino! These sins were accumulating in
my personal file (remember Oberhausen 1961), and I began to
experience difficulties over arranging trips abroad.

The 30th USSR Championship was held at the end of 1962. The
entry was rather uneven, weaker than usual. My rivals were Tal,
Spassky, Taimanov and Stein. I managed to beat Stein, Spassky
and Tal in our individual encounters (games 28–30), and although
I spoiled things at the finish, scoring only 2 points out of 5, I
managed to hang on to first place. It will not be out of place to recall
how the prize-winners were rewarded in the USSR Championships,
which were stronger than most international tournaments. There
were only three prizes – of 300, 200 and 100 roubles. However,
the prizes were not published, but were arranged by a secret
department of the Sports Committee, and since there was no
publicity, there was no control. For my victory in the 1962 USSR
Championship, I was sent 225 roubles, before tax!

To be fair, it should be mentioned that the efforts of Fischer and
his deputy in the Soviet Union, Karpov, have not gone to waste,
and last year the Council of Ministers decreed that the rates should
be raised slightly. Thus in the 1975 USSR Championship the first
prize was 400 roubles (and the number of prizes was also increased,
as far as I know).

I have already said that, although I was USSR Champion, I had
difficulty in travelling abroad. Evidently, apart from the official

organs, I was also being hindered by one of the powerful grand-masters. The Chess Federation had fixed up a visit by Keres and myself to a tournament in the USA [the 1963 Piatigorsky Cup – ed.], but Petrosian insisted on his participation in the tournament instead of me. The Americans sent tickets for three participants, but to no avail. It was only the two of them, Keres and Petrosian, who went.

Then a visit to Cuba was planned for me. To all appearances, it too was being wrecked. Then I had a stroke of luck: at that time a tournament between large factories was being held in Moscow by the sports society 'Trud', of which I had been a member for a long time. A large group of old chess-playing production workers sent a letter to the USSR Sports Committee, demanding that I should be allowed to compete abroad. 'The voice of the masses', public opinion, sometimes has a role to play in the Soviet Union. I was sent to Cuba.

The tournament proved to be a difficult one for me. In view of the uneven strength of the participants, it was necessary to win game after game, in order to have a chance of first place. The tropical heat, and unusual playing conditions were very tiring. During the second half of the tournament I lost to one of my main rivals, Geller. Then I fell into a hopeless position against Wade. I was a rook down, and only serious time trouble could to some extent excuse the fact that I didn't resign. But in a comparatively simple position, Wade began complicating matters unnecessarily, and blundered away his queen for a rook, after which I managed, with difficulty, to win the ending. After the game I asked my opponent why he hadn't chosen one of the several simple winning paths available to him, 'Against you', he replied, 'I wanted to win most exactly.' I managed to win from another difficult position, against Letelier, and I finished up in first place. I have talked only about the difficult moments which I recall, but there were also some good games. By a temporary queen sacrifice, I won against Robatsch (game 31); utilizing what was then an unusual scheme of development, I defeated Trifunović as black (game 32). Trifunović's reputation as an invincible drawing master was widely known, and so after the tournament I sent my notes on this game to a Yugoslav chess journal, with the heading: 'How to Beat Trifunović'.

Scoring 16 points out of 21, I finished half a point ahead of Geller, Pachman and Tal. The tournament proved exhausting. The unfamiliar tropical climate, the harmful smoking of cigars. . . . Two months later, I fell seriously ill, for the first time in my life, with a stomach ulcer. I was not up to playing chess, but was obliged to play in the 31st USSR Championship, which was to have been a world championship zonal. During the tournament I had to take medicine and tranquillizers. I did not play brilliantly, but better than I had feared, and managed to win several subtle games, in particular against Suetin and Polugayevsky (games 33–34). With two rounds to go my chances of ending up amongst the winners were quite good: all I needed were another $1\frac{1}{2}$ points. But for the only time in my life I collapsed at the finish, and lost both games. The illness told in the end.

After the Championship, a special Zonal Tournament was arranged, as a qualifying event for the Interzonal. It was to be made up of the six highest placed in the Championship, plus two personally invited players (on the basis of previous successes). The seventh particpant named was Smyslov, who had not taken part in the Championship (it was for his sake that this whole system had been thought up), and for the eighth the Chess Federation nominated me. Literally a few days before the start of the tournament there was a surprising turn of events. Smyslov put in an application to the Federation, requesting that he be allowed to have one of the four USSR qualifying places and go directly into the Interzonal. The Federation rejected his claim. He then turned to his friends with access to the Government and leading Party Organs. From there – from above – came an order which was un-conditionally accepted by the USSR Sports Committee, and the head of the Chess Federation (at that time Rodionov) was reprimanded.

From this incident the reader can gain an idea of the bureaucratic hierarchy of the heads of sport, in particular of chess.

The USSR Chess Federation, a public organ with the right of consultative vote, is controlled by the USSR Sports Committee. Supervision of the activities of the Sports Committee is carried out by corresponding departments in the Communist Party Central Committee. Even higher, in the Communist Party Central Committee's Politburo, there is a man who is responsible for sport, including chess. At that time this man was the present Minister of Culture (demoted from the Gods to a mere mortal!) Demichev. Evidently it was he who heeded Smyslov's call, and in an instant decided the matter in favour of the capricious grandmaster.

There was no limit to the indignation of the competitors in the Zonal Tournament. It was decided to call a strike and refuse to play. However, the strike was vetoed by Spassky (strongly influenced by Bondarevsky). With such a small number of participants it had to be unanimous and as a result the conspiracy broke up. A pity!

Knowing about this incident, chess followers will now be able to guess why, at the Biel Interzonal Tournament in 1976, Kuzmin was replaced by Smyslov.

The Zonal Tournament was extremely strong, and since I had not made the grade in the USSR Championship, I felt not quite equal with the other competitors. For success in a strong tournament, a player needs to believe in his lucky star. Here I had no luck. First I lost to Holmov after a bad blunder, then I was brilliantly crushed by Bronstein. His example was followed by Stein, and just before the end, when only a win against Spassky would do – even the penultimate round did not help – I lost to him. As a result I scored less than 50%, a slight consolation being my two wins over Geller.

In September I took part in a strong tournament in Belgrade. I played unevenly but shared second place with Ivkov. First place was taken by Spassky without any difficulty. I think that 1964–65 were the years of Spassky's best form, and after seeing his play in Belgrade, I was not at all surprised by his victories in the Candidates' Matches the following year . . .

At the end of 1964 the 32nd USSR Championship was held in Kiev, where I had normally played fairly well. On this occasion I excelled even myself. I took first place without difficulty, defeating my main rivals, Bronstein and Tal (game 35). Among the eleven games that I won were several clear-cut victories, such as those against Vasyukov, Sakharov and Lutikov (games 36–38). Some of the games were decided right in the opening stages. It would seem that I had reached maturity as a chess player. I could only regret the fact that I had played the previous year's championship and the subsequent Zonal Tournament in a state of depression. In later interviews I would frequently recall this world championship cycle, and how it had worked out badly for me, since I considered that this would have been the most suitable period for me to battle for the World Championship. Besides my chess maturity, I was also in the peak of condition competitively.

Over the ten years that I had been a grandmaster, my chess style had undergone significant changes. But what they wrote about me was just the same as before. In 1960, when I first became USSR champion, the journalist V. Vasiliev interviewed me, and then wrote an article entitled 'The Bishop Move', which became widely known. I told Vasiliev that I valued highly the art of defence in chess, that I saw an unusual form of romanticism in this, and that for my successes I was chiefly indebted to my ability to save difficult positions. From that time, right to the present day, all this has been cited in numerous publications. But meanwhile a man, even at a mature age, is capable of changing his views. There came a time when I realized that the ability to defend was – for a good chess player – insufficient. You can't be dependent upon your opponent's will, but must try to impose your will on him. I realized that I was restricting my possibilities both as a person and as a chess player.

From childhood I had known how to defend, and nothing more. I had to relearn, and to a certain extent I was successful. I would put down my successes in the 1960s, and my rise in stature as a chess player, to the fact that I learned how to fight for the initiative and to maintain it. Even now I do not consider this to be my forte, but I succeeded in developing my feeling for the initiative to a considerable extent. My play became, without a doubt, more diverse. In 1965, I, together with Spassky, was called one of the most versatile grandmasters in the world.

In this championship I had practically assured myself of first place three rounds before the finish. The result was I beat Bronstein into second place by three points.

During this Championship I had received an invitation to play in the so-called 'Peace Tournament' in Zagreb, and in a television interview straight after the event I spoke of my desire to take part in it. But the Chess Federation authorities informed me that soon, within ten days, I had to go to Hungary. Any normal person can appreciate that it is possible to play in Hungary in February, and in Yugoslavia in April. But in the Soviet Union the average grandmaster is allowed a maximum of two international tournaments a year, so it was clear that if I went to Hungary I would not make the Yugoslav tournament. But I wanted to go to Yugoslavia, since a strong tournament with good prizes was planned there. And since I was USSR Champion, I was strongly resolved to stick up for my rights. I was invited to talk it over with the Deputy Chairman of the USSR Sports Committee. I recall this conversation very well. He told me that J. Kadar himself had requested that I should play in Hungary. He said: 'You know that in 1956 Soviet tanks smashed holes in the houses of Budapest. You have been selected to, as it were, plug up these holes – by your cultural co-operation!' This was very graphically stated, and *so* understandable. But I dug my heels in, and refused. My conduct was discussed at a session of the Chess Federation, who issued a reprimand, and temporarily stopped me from going abroad.

Thus I was not allowed to play in Yugoslavia. And the authorities essentially achieved what they wanted, since in the summer of the same year I was sent to a tournament in Hungary, in Gyula.

I managed to travel there with my wife. For mere mortals such a possibility is entirely ruled out, but for a chess player it is sometimes possible. I recall a story told by Rostropovich. Gilels, who was preparing a lengthy tour, sent a request to the Minister of Culture, Furtseva: 'Since I am a sick man and require nursing, I ask that I be sent abroad together with my wife.' Rostropovich, who was also planning to go abroad, on hearing about Gilels' letter, sent in his own request: 'Since I am a perfectly healthy person, I ask that I be sent abroad together with my wife!'

The tournament in Gyula was not very strong, and in addition I had my share of luck. I managed to score $14\frac{1}{2}$ out of 15.

In August an international tournament was held in Yerevan. On the whole, international tournaments in the Soviet union are pretty rare. Smaller chess nations such as Yugoslavia and Spain hold six to eight international tournaments a year, whereas the mightiest chess power rarely manages three. As is known, such a tournament can be made up of half local players, and the rest foreigners.* It is by no means an easy matter to entice the other half of the competitors into the Soviet Union. Soviet players are strong, and the prizes poor. With rare exceptions, the prizes are in the local currency, roubles, and roubles cannot be exchanged for other currencies. If you add that the service in the Soviet Union is 'by no means good', i.e. simply bad, then it is clear that the foreign chess player in the Soviet Union can neither make enough money, nor gain any pleasure.

It is no accident that a player who once plays in a tournament in the USSR rarely wishes to return. The Federations of Bulgaria,

---

* Now the requirement has been reduced to one third foreigners (ed.).

Czechoslovakia and Hungary, as if fulfilling a labour conscription, sent their grandmasters in turn to the Soviet Union at the request of the Soviet Federation. But even so, tournaments frequently collapse on account of the non-arrival of the foreign competitors.

There are, however, exceptions. What you can certainly find in the Soviet Union is good chess, and from this one can learn. And there are players who forget about all the inconveniences, and come to the USSR as to a chess course. One such strange chap is grandmaster Robert Byrne. If you examine his success curve, you will see that his participation in international tournaments in Moscow helps him to regain his best form.

But let's return to the international tournament in Yerevan. After my victories in the USSR Championship, and especially at Gyula, I was the clear favourite, despite the participation of the world champion, Petrosian. And that's how it worked out.

I played easily and efficiently, and soon drew away from my rivals. The world champion had Black against me. He was already by no means the player of the years 1962–63. On ascending to the throne, he gave up chess, and decided to supplement his education. On the eve of his match with Botvinnik, he did not even have a secondary school leaving diploma, whereas at the end of 1965 he had already defended his dissertation for the title of Candidate in Philosophical Sciences. In our game, Petrosian succeeded in equalizing easily, but that is all, and without any particular complications it ended in a draw. The result of the tournament was that I took first place, two points ahead of Petrosian and Stein.

That year I was to meet Petrosian again. This was in the traditional Leningrad–Moscow match, where I won both games (games 39–40).

These games had a beneficial effect on Petrosian. He realized just how seriously he had to prepare for the coming match with Spassky, but for me the opposite was true. It seemed to me that I was now clearly stronger than everyone else, and that I should easily come first wherever I played. But in fact this was of course not so, as I was soon forced to accept.

In the 33rd championship of the country in Tallinn (end of 1965), my troubles came thick and fast. They began with a defeat by Keres. I always found it difficult playing against him, and this game, which he conducted with youthful energy, was perhaps the best of his four wins against me. With characteristic enthusiasm, I began to pick up, but isolated wins alternated with stinging defeats, and as a result I did not manage to rise above the 50% zone.

Upset, I agreed to play in a training tournament organized by Petrosian to give him' practical preparation for his match with Spassky. In this tournament I again played weakly, scoring less than 50%.

These tournaments were a good lesson for me. They showed that I still had to work more deeply on the game.

* 10 *

Two Hard Years

The second half of 1966 was a favourable time for me. I played in a tournament in Bucharest, winning eleven games, and drawing three. Then I played quite well in the USSR–Yugoslavia match at Sukhumi. At the end of the summer I won an international tournament at Sochi with 11½ points out of 15, half a point ahead of Polugayevsky. I again performed quite well in the USSR team championship, where I represented the 'Trud' Sporting Society on second board behind Botvinnik. This was the last event in which Botvinnik demonstrated his amazing understanding of chess. Along with many chess fans, I recall very well his sparkling wins over Smyslov and Keres. I scored 7½ out of 10, without losing a game.

Later in the year I played for the USSR team in the Olympiad in Havana. It should be said that my absence from the teams in 1962 and 1964 was no accident. Within the Soviet Union there is serious competition for places in the Olympiad team. For victory in the Olympiad, the Sports Committee pays a considerable bonus in Soviet currency – 1500 roubles – so that there are plenty who want to take part. In addition, there were serious difficulties with regard to my personal file, on account of my previous conduct abroad.

In 1965 I joined the Communist Party. I was under the naive impression that, by my participation in party work, I could correct much that I did not like. I also realized that it would make it easier for me to travel abroad.

In Havana the Soviet team found itself competing with the Americans, headed by Fischer. It is known that Fischer was unable to play on Friday evenings or Saturdays, and the Americans asked that they should be met half way if important matches should happen to fall on these days. The match with the Soviets fell on one of these days, but the leaders of the USSR team refused to make any concessions. It was clear that the Americans would not play without Fischer, but the match was arranged for the normal time. The Americans failed to appear, and it was announced that the match had concluded with a score of 4–0 in favour of the USSR. A major scandal blew up. For the first time in many years, American chess players had succeeded in breaking the cultural blockade of Cuba organized by the USA, but, instead of being shown gratitude, they were not allowed to play the individual encounter under normal conditions against the Soviet team, whom they were chasing. We debated this question several times inside our own circle. The team captain Syerov would listen only to Bondarevsky, who, as I have already said, is not exactly flexible. I spoke up several times, saying that we should make concessions, but no one would support me. Genuine political or social activity by citizens is not highly valued in the Soviet Union, and here this became very clear: Tal, Stein, Polugayevsky, Spassky and Petrosian all kept silent. In the end, instructions from Moscow were awaited. The match eventually took place on a day specially set aside by the Cubans. It was a tense match, and concluded in a victory for the Soviet team by the minimum margin, $2\frac{1}{2}$–$1\frac{1}{2}$. On top board Spassky was very badly placed against Fischer, but managed to save the half point. I am afraid that Spassky failed to draw the necessary conclusions from this game. One sensed that Fischer was developing into a very powerful force. But Spassky thought that with his expertise in defence, and his ability to lead an opponent into a sharp, intuitive struggle, he had nothing to fear.

At the Havana Olympiad I played quite well, and made the best score on board five. As a rule, team events are more tiring than individual ones, although the opposition may be weaker. Team meetings, communal analysis, the strict timetable with no special days for adjournments, irregular meals (since often 500 people require feeding simultaneously, and are thereby forced to wait for hours) – all this leads to extreme tiredness. I consider that the chess olympiad, in the form in which it has been held for the last two decades, has become obsolete, and the International Chess Federation is right to seek new ways of conducting World Championship team events.

A month after the Olympiad, although still very tired, I had to play in the 34th USSR Championship in Tbilisi, also a qualifying tournament for the World Championship. Considering that I am on the whole an active player, I won very few games in that Championship. I scored seventeen draws – all of them fighting ones – and accidentally won four games. As a result I shared third place with Gipslis and Taimanov, and had to play a further three-man tournament with them for the right to participate in the Interzonal. As a result of the play-off it was Taimanov who dropped out.

In the summer of 1967, international tournaments, dedicated to the 50th anniversary of Soviet power, were held with great pomp in Moscow and Leningrad. The Moscow event was highly imposing, with large prizes – for the first time in the Soviet Union a prize of 2000 roubles was put up. The rumour went round that Fischer had asked to take part – without any extra appearance fee! – but that he had not been admitted. It would indeed have been a disgrace to let an American win a tournament dedicated to the anniversary of such a commemorative date!

The tournament in Leningrad was rather weaker and less imposing. I was allotted to play there, in my home town. I played strongly, and won a number of good games. One of them, against Udovčić (game 41), was highly rated by that master of attack, Keres. By winning ten games and drawing six I came first, one point ahead of Holmov in second place.

At the end of the summer, the USSR–Yugoslavia match was again held, only this time it was arranged in the form of an all-play-all tournament. Without great difficulty, I managed to take first place here as well.

The Interzonal Tournament at Sousse in Tunisia was due to begin in October. From time to time my ulcer had been troubling me, and the latest attack occurred just two weeks before the start of it. I lay in bed at home, stuck to a special diet, gave up smoking, and arrived at the tournament somewhat weakened. For the past few years my trainer had been Furman, but he had recently undergone a serious stomach operation, and so I engaged the assistance of Vasyukov, a diligent and hard-working man. But his chess repertoire was quite different to mine, and during the course of the tournament, in order to adapt mutually, each of us had to do some relearning. After a bad start, I again began smoking. All these changes had a bad effect on my play, and I trudged along around the 50% mark. In the lead was Fischer, having won brilliantly against Reshevsky, Stein, and many other grandmasters. My game against him ended in a draw after an interesting struggle, but that was one of the last games that he played in the tournament. For reasons that I still do not fully understand, he walked out of the tournament – a very rare occurrence in chess. It is usually the back markers who, 'for health reasons', leave tournaments. On the whole I consider that Fischer's actions have often coincided with the demands of the chess world, but that Fischer himself has never, in the past or now, considered the fact that he belongs to the chess world and is responsible to it: he has no right to hide his talent.

At the finish I at last picked up. With a certain amount of tournament fortune I won in turn against Portisch, Barczay (game 42), Bilek, Miagmasuren and Cuellar. I recall how, when I began my game with Miagmasuren (game 43), I was surprised at the exemplary way in which he played the opening, and the thought suddenly occurred to me that he had been prepared for the game by a Soviet player. However, there is nothing surprising in this. At each Interzonal there are a number of Soviet trainers, and they do not have all that much of their 'own' work. I knew that Gufeld had prepared Miagmasuren for his game with Fischer. But the idea that the Soviets could collectively work against me too seemed totally unnatural, until I encountered it at the board. In the end I shared second place with Geller and Gligorić, behind Larsen, the winner of the tournament.

The prize-giving ceremony remains clearly in my memory. The representatives of western countries received their prizes in Swiss francs, whereas the Eastern Bloc players received theirs in Tunisian dinars, a currency which can be exchanged in practically no other country. Great was our disappointment, but the tournament organizers were implacable. It must be said that in the Soviet Union they met us half way and made an exception, exchanging our dinars for certificates – valuable pieces of paper, which inside the Soviet Union are valued no less than convertible currency.

* 11 *

1968: a Brilliant Year

Early in 1968 I went off to play in Holland at the Wijk aan Zee Tournament. This was the first time for many years that I had been to an international tournament in a capitalist country. Such tournaments, where the prizes are in convertible currency, are especially valued, and only the top grandmasters gain the opportunity to play in them. The conditions were unusual for me, in that there were two adjournment sessions a day. On the whole I tend to have lots of adjourned games, and here at the very start I adjourned against Padevski, a game which was to continue almost to move 100, and each day I found myself working nine hours, not including preparations for the following round. What are trade unions for in this enlightened twentieth century? One round gave way to another, and all the time I was playing on the same adjourned game, winning each new encounter on the way! The situation cleared up after a week, when I had scored 7 out of 7. The eighth game was with Tal (game 44). Away from the board we were on friendly terms, and the tournament was going indifferently for him. I felt sorry for him, but we had to make a game of it, especially since everyone around expected us to agree a quick draw. Tal played the first part of the game accurately, and gained approximate equality, but then made a mistake. I managed to open up the position to my advantage, and win the game. It was only on the following day that I had my first draw, with Donner.

In this series of seven wins there were several good games. Before this, in the Interzonal, I had played badly against the Yugoslavs, scoring only one point out of four. Here I gained my revenge, winning against Ivkov, Matanović, Ciric and Karaklajić. I consider my game with Matanović (game 45) to be one of the best achievements in my life in the field of chess strategy. With 10½ points out of 11, I was heading for a new record in the tournament, but in round twelve, with the better position against Portisch, I blundered away a piece. The tournament lost interest for me, and I drew the remaining three games without a fight. Even so, it wasn't too bad: I scored 12 points out of 15, three points ahead of Tal, Portisch and Hort.

Then I began preparing for my quarter-final candidates' match against Reshevsky. Up till then I had played only two games against him, both of them had ended in draws. I remembered our game from the 1960 Buenos Aires tournament, which had taken place on a Friday. At Reshevsky's request, we had played in the morning in order to finish before sunset, which in the Argentinian winter meant up to two o'clock in the afternoon. In the course of the session Reshevsky clearly outplayed me, and at exactly two o'clock he began thinking about his sealed move. There were two possible continuations: one move won a pawn, but gave White drawing chances, while the other did not lead to a material gain, but maintained all the advantages of Black's position, and was the stronger. Reshevsky grew nervous, and kept looking at the clock. After thirteen minutes he sealed his move, which turned out to be not the best, and I managed to save the game. This game later proved decisive in the battle for first place which we eventually shared.

In preparing for Reshevsky, I pinned my hopes on my better practical know-how, and on my superior knowledge of modern opening theory. I realized that I was up against a subtle strategic player, whose knowledge of the subtleties of the game was probably superior to mine. I would have to curb Reshevsky's onslaught with the white pieces. Furman was back as my trainer and we prepared some solid systems for Black, with several interesting ideas for White.

The match was played in Amsterdam in May, and was essentially decided in the first two games. The first game, in which Reshevsky was White, went in his favour. In the opening he outplayed me, and obtained a strategically won position. But he evidently underestimated my tactical ability, played too sharply, and made a couple of tactical mistakes, so that I was able to save the half point. In the second game I opened 1 e4, which I play rather infrequently. I knew the first fifteen moves that Reshevsky would play, and had prepared an interesting continuation, which was new at that time. I played those fifteen moves, even eighteen, in one and a half minutes, whereas in his usual way, Reshevsky, being in addition rather rusty, spent about an hour over them. In a practical game a large difference in time is highly unpleasant, and plays on the nerves of the one who is behind the clock. And indeed, Reshevsky became nervous, began playing more quickly, and, on emerging from the opening, he blundered away a pawn. The game was decided, although Reshevsky dragged it out until the adjournment, when he then resigned without resuming. In a short match, an advantage in points to one of the players is highly unpleasant to the other, and especially so here, since Reshevsky had suffered two psychological blows one after another. The third game quickly ended in a draw. In the fourth I adopted a novel set-up (game 46). Reshevsky equalized, but I played more rationally and more quickly than my opponent. Reshevsky began to run short of time, and, anticipating time trouble, started playing more quickly. In a relatively simple, equal endgame position he made several mistakes and lost. The fifth game, where for a long time I was in difficulties, ended in a draw, and then in the sixth I again won. Reshevsky played the opening rather flippantly, I gained a big advantage, and confidently converted it into a win. This was my best game of the match. In the next two games I held the advantage, but both ended in draws, and I won the match by a score of 5½–2½. Reshevsky was upset, and did not even come to the closing ceremony. This, however, is understandable: it must have been painful for him, at his age, to lose a match without a struggle.

I was now faced with the semi-final match against Tal to be played in Moscow. Prior to the match the psychological situation was rather strange. After all, I had won practically every game I had played against Tal, and even the colours had made no difference. I realized that, when playing against me in tournaments, Tal took risks, trying to get even with me for the indignities suffered, and that in a match he would be much more cautious, since it was the result of the match as a whole that was important, and not just individual games. During the short time available I prepared myself as well as possible theoretically, but psychologically, as it turned out, I was not ready for a serious struggle against him. At the start of the match Tal began playing closed openings against me, in which he is not a great expert. On the other hand, the character of the play was quieter, and no doubt he wanted first of all to draw several games, so as to gain self-confidence. In the very first game I rather underestimated my opponent, and went into a very difficult pawn ending. It was amazing that Tal failed to win it. The second game quickly ended in a draw, Tal having confidently equalized. Then in the third game Tal caught me in a prepared variation. Though I thought over one move for 100 minutes (!), I nevertheless failed to find sufficient counterplay. My position started going downhill, especially since I was in time trouble right from the opening. But the miraculous occurred: Tal failed to find a winning continuation, and I was able to take play into a rook ending a pawn down. It was probaly still lost, but Tal was too uncertain of his endgame technique to win such a position.

Soon after the third game, as I later found out, Tal's personal doctor arrived in Moscow. Tal certainly has troubles with his health, but to have a personal doctor – such a thing just isn't done in the Soviet Union. At the start of the fourth game, Tal was a few minutes late, and, on greeting me, appeared somewhat embarrassed. I somehow associated this moment with the arrival of his doctor. Play began. In this game I adopted one of my prepared lines. Tal did not manage to resolve things at the board, in addition thought for twenty-five to thirty minutes over each move, and was soon in time trouble. His position was very difficult, but here I had a recurrence of my old weakness, and at the first opportunity won a pawn, thus losing, as it turned out, all my advantage. A draw seemed imminent, but in time trouble Tal blundered and lost.

In the next game (game 47) Tal attempted to pull one back. He began with his favourite 1 e4. In a Ruy Lopez he was rather slow in organizing pressure on the black position; I managed to seize the initiative and won quickly. The match seemed to be decided. I held an imposing lead, and had the white pieces in the next game. I remembered that I could and should be pressing Tal in every game. I obtained an advantage in this game, but ran short of time, allowed my opponent the opportunity to seize the initiative by an exchange sacrifice, and lost. Incidentally, during the match I had two seconds: Furman and Osnos. Just before the sixth game Furman, who was a member of the Central Army Sports Club, was unexpectedly called away to Leningrad to take part in some insignificant team event. This incident disturbed me, but at the time I couldn't think of any real reason why anyone should want to damage my chances.

The loss of that game, and the departure of my main helper – all this put the match in jeopardy. I took the decision (perhaps incorrectly) to settle for draws in the remaining games – this decision was quite in accordance with my confused state of mind at that point. At the same time I took a further step. Tal's doctor was all the time in the hall, and never took his eyes off the board at which we were playing. More accurately, he did not disturb me, but all the time kept Tal in his field of vision. I suspected that Tal was taking drugs before the games. From the point of view of the FIDE rules, there was nothing illegal in this. It no doubt helped Tal, although it is known that drugs lower a person's will-power. In view of this, I thought that the doctor was exerting a visual influence on Tal during the game, and was reassuring him. I consider that this hypothesis of mine may well have a scientific basis. Without expressing my views, I wrote a letter to the control team, with the request that the doctor, who was sitting very close to the stage, should be moved back to the eighth row. The Tal camp – his assistants and he himself – were unhappy about the action I had taken, but the control team fulfilled my request. However, there is nothing unusual in this; matches for the World Championship with the participation of Fischer were, on his demand, conducted in the same way.

In the seventh game I chose a dubious opening variation, and straight from the opening went into a difficult ending, where for the full five hours I had to struggle for a draw by finding the only saving moves. In the eighth game I held a positional advantage, but it too ended in a draw. Again in the ninth game I chose an unpretentious opening variation. I equalized, and even gained a slight advantage, which proved insufficient to win. There remained just one game, where I had White. Tal, of course, had to play for a win, and he chose a sharp variation of the Dutch Defence. I was not at my best in that game. I gained an advantage, but avoided all complicated continuations, trying to simplify the position (in this lies the psychological vulnerability of a player who is aiming for a draw, especially if he is used to playing for a win). By move 25 I was already losing. In the time scramble Tal was insufficiently energetic, or rather he gave up a pawn without sufficient justification, and left me some drawing chances. In what was still a difficult position, I sealed a move which, as it later turned out, was not expected by Tal. True, he afterwards maintained that after the best sealed move he had no winning chances. On the other hand, I made a thorough study of the position after the move actually sealed. The two opponents spent a sleepless night analysing, and the next day came the tense, nerve-racking resumption. I had, of course, been able to analyse the position more deeply. After three hours' play we agreed to a draw, and I thus went forward to the Final Candidates' Match.

Immediately after the match, I gave an interview for the newspaper *Shakhmatnaya Moskva*. Dissatisfied with my play, I also spoke disapprovingly of my opponent, calling him the 'great routine' player. There was some justification in me personally making such an assessment, especially since I had noticed the stereotyped natures of Tal's attacking play back in 1957. Tal had, and still has, many fans. His uncompromising style of play delights chess enthusiasts, and they are won over by his desire and ability to take risks and even bluff his way through. At the same time, Tal's skill in building up his game is inadequate, and is often based on routine assessments and routine methods. I consider the genuine masters of attack to be Alekhine, Keres and Spassky.

I now had shortly to do battle with Spassky, who up to then had easily won his matches against Geller and Larsen. But the style of his victories in 1968 was different, less convincing than in 1965, when one after another he had crushed Keres, Geller and Tal. In 1968 he appeared intentionally to neglect modern opening theory, and, so it seemed, did not try to outplay his opponents, but rather waited for them to beat themselves. Of course, the middle game was Spassky's main strength, and here he was inimitable, but I considered that, with my understanding, knowledge and technique, I could compete with him on equal terms.

I prepared for the match with Furman, but it turned out that Furman couldn't go with me to Kiev, where the match was to be held. The authorities of the Central Army Sports Club would not release him. At that time I did not realize which way the wind was blowing; the absurdity of the situation was obvious, but there was nothing to be done. I was angry with Spassky, since I thought that it was one of the tricks of his trainer, Bondarevsky, but, as it turned out, neither Spassky nor Bondarevsky had anything to do with this incident. It was Petrosian's doing. The World Champion, having beaten Spassky in 1966, was not afraid of him, whereas the prospect of a match with me was unpleasant for him. In order to render me impotent, through his friends in the army – in particular the ageing

Marshal Bagramian – he managed to put pressure on the Central Army Sports Club. First Furman was sent away during my match with Tal, and then he was forbidden to accompany me to the Final Match. It could be objected that there were other trainers apart from Furman, and indeed I soon began playing successfully without him, but at that moment it was highly unpleasant for me.

I began the match against Spassky in a psychologically depressed state, and even my superior theoretical preparation could not compensate for this. In addition, I played badly in the second game on account of an unfortunate incident (the first game ended in a draw). On the whole, I am not inclined to blame my chess failures on external factors, but this was highly exceptional. Normally, I am not distracted while playing, especially since my hearing is impaired. But here I suddenly felt the building shaking. In 1967 there had been a landslip in Kiev, when a whole block on the banks of the Dnieper had been destroyed, and I thought that this must be the start of an earthquake. I became very agitated, and made several blunders to lose from a level position literally within a few moves. It was only after this that I stood up and asked what was happening. 'It's a salute', I was told, 'for tank crew members' day.' It turned out that for forty minutes there had been firing by several hundred guns!

The third game, in which I had Black, ended in a draw, although Spassky was pushed to neutralize my spatial advantage. But in the fourth game, Spassky with Black quite outplayed me. On achieving a completely won position, he did not hasten to force matters, aiming instead to adjourn the game and find the most effective winning path. In doing this he relaxed his vigilance, and overlooked a strong counter-blow. Unfortunately, I did not notice it immediately, and only after making my move did I see it, when I almost cried. The game was adjourned, and Spassky showed good technique in converting his advantage into a win. The fifth game ended in a draw. The following day I decided to attempt to change the course of the match. I had prepared an interesting continuation in the Queen's Gambit involving queen-side castling (game 48). In general, Spassky senses fairly keenly the turning points during a game. After thinking for more than forty minutes over his move, he found a very fine continuation. He sacrificed a piece, which I could not avoid taking, but as a result I came under a formidable attack. Subtly and unhurriedly, Spassky developed his offensive. Hard as I tried, I was unable to obtain any serious counter-play. I had to return the piece, but this did not halt the attack. However, we both ran desperately short of time, and here, as last, Spassky overlooked a powerful tactical stroke. When the smoke had cleared following the time scramble, White had a considerable material advantage, sufficient to win.

I felt that this was a decisive psychological turning point. In the past Spassky had reacted badly to a defeat, and when the next game began, and Spassky changed his favourite e4 for the more rarely adopted d4, I decided that I must at all costs involve him in a tactical battle. But in fact I was seeing the situation as if in a distorting mirror. At that time Spassky was already a more hardened fighter than ten years before, and it was I who was nervous, being anxious to eliminate Spassky's lead. To the astonishment of my seconds, I chose the King's Indian defence, an opening which I play extremely rarely, and then only against weak opponents. Spassky played splendidly in that game. In the Sämisch Variation he introduced an interesting innovation, and, being inexperienced in the King's Indian, which I prefer to play against White, I failed to resolve the position. Spassky obtained an attack in the centre and on the king-side, and ended the game with a mate.

The match was already Spassky's, this was clear. I played the following games indifferently, failed to perceive the moment when Spassky seized the initiative, and lost it too. In the ninth game I succeeded in worrying my opponent and his second, who had already bought his ticket home. To escape from my positional pressure, Spassky was forced to sacrifice the exchange, and his second had to return his ticket to the booking office. But everything turned out all right: there was sufficient compensation for the sacrificed material, and on resumption Spassky was able to draw. The tenth and last game also ended in a draw with the advantage on Spassky's side, and thus the overall score in the match was $6\frac{1}{2}$–$3\frac{1}{2}$ in my opponent's favour. This was a crushing win, and in an interview given by Spassky, one sensed that he too was surprised at the ease with which he had won the Final Candidates' Match.

In the world team championship, held in Lugano in the autumn of 1968 the USSR team took first place without difficulty. And I played quite well, achieving the best results on board three. In November, together with Petrosian and Spassky, I went off to play in Majorca. On this occasion the trip was arranged for me by Petrosian. He was planning to have me as his trainer.

At the end of my stay in Switzerland, I had suffered a recurrence of my ulcer trouble. I spent ten days at home on a diet, and it seemed that I would find things difficult in Palma. But I was saved by my theoretical knowledge, which I had specially prepared for the Candidates' Matches, and had not been able to use. I played exceptionally confidently throughout this tournament, and towards the finish defeated both of my main rivals, Larsen and Spassky (games 49–50).

This was a familiar situation to me. Not long before the return match between Tal and Botvinnik, I had defeated Botvinnik. Before the 1966 match between Spassky and Petrosian, I had flattened Petrosian. I recall that, on adjourning a pawn up in my game against Spassky, I went up to Petrosian, and said: 'There's nothing you can do about it, Spassky will be World Champion!' 'Why, what do you mean?', asked Petrosian, looking disconcerted. 'Well, I'm beating him!' I concluded. Petrosian winced and swallowed hard. After this conversation there could be no question of my being his second. And my prophecy came true.

In the tournament I scored fourteen out of seventeen, easily outscoring ten or so top-class grandmasters. Along with Wijk aan Zee 1968, this was one of the best tournaments of my life.

* 12 *

1969–70: Decline

After the year 1968 my success curve began to fall, although I didn't appreciate this straight away. At first, in the spring of 1969, I won a tournament in Sarajevo with a good result – 12 out of 15 – and then one in Czechoslovakia with 11½ out of 15. In the summer I played in a fairly weak tournament in Leningrad, under the ostentatious name of the 'Championship of the All-union Central Trade Union Council'. Perhaps it was because I hadn't played against Soviet masters for a long time, but at any rate in the semi-final of this event I felt an extreme lack of confidence. 'Perhaps', I thought, 'in view of my past successes, the organizers should have invited me directly into the final. But what a disgrace! I may not even get through.' After a struggle and many anxious moments I nevertheless made the final. There I found it easier, and took first place.

I found things even more difficult in my next tournament, in Havana. Battling for the leadership with Gligorić and Suetin, I lost crushingly to Gligorić as White, and drew with difficulty as White against Suetin. After many anxious moments I managed to catch up with Suetin in the last round, to share first with him.

This was to be my last success for a long time. At the end of the year I again played in Majorca, where the entry was stronger and more even than in 1968. After dropping several full and half points on the way, I shared third place with Hort, behind the winner, Larsen, and Petrosian. True, the world champion, Spassky, could only come fifth. Of the games played in Majorca, the only one I could be pleased about was my victory over Mecking (game 51), with whom I had already had a score to settle. Two years earlier, in Tunisia, I had suffered a vexing defeat at the hands of this young player. Now, calling upon my erudition and experience, I lured Mecking into a variation unfamiliar to him, and won first the opening battle, and, after a short resistance, the game as well.

The Match 'USSR v. The Rest of the World', organized in Yugoslavia in the spring of 1970, was a unique event in world chess. The army of Soviet chess players is enormous, and very strong. The USSR team could probably compete with a World team on as many as fifty boards, as is shown by the matches between the Russian Federation and Hungary, Ukraine–Bulgaria, or White Russia–DDR, where little-known masters without any international titles win against players of world renown. For how can they gain these international titles, when travel abroad is restricted, and only a handful out of this vast army have the chance and the right to demonstrate their chess strength abroad? Besides, that modest organization, the USSR Sports Committee, arranges thirty per cent of all business trips abroad by Soviet citizens.

In the USSR, preparations were made for the match: a training camp was set up, and the best trainers were enlisted. But there was no harmony between the team members. Rather there was just the opposite – clashes of opinion, disagreements and arguments. The antagonism between the participants became especially acute when the board order was announced, after being worked out by the sports committee following consultations with the experts. The bottom boards in the team were given to the oldest players. I consider that, in a team with such reserves as Stein and Bronstein, the players could have been arranged in almost any order. Probably all, with the exception of the World Champion, should have been placed strictly in order of age, after announcing this beforehand.

It turned out that the Rest of the World Team was more united and harmonious than the Soviets. What's more, I remember how during play some of the Soviet players walked up and down the stage, rejoicing over the misfortunes of their own team members. The atmosphere within the team was nervy, and did not lend itself to serious play. It was perhaps for this reason that in my games against Portisch I allowed myself to open 1 e4, and that also in one of the games I forgot to make an obvious pawn move in the opening, and allowed the exchange of my 'Spanish' bishop for Black's queen's knight. By that time Portisch had developed into the strongest player in Eastern Europe, of which his encounter with me was a further indication. He won our individual match by a score of $2\frac{1}{2}$–$1\frac{1}{2}$, and, incidentally, in the last round he agreed to a draw in a position where he was the exchange up, and where he could have coped perfectly well with his time trouble. I gained the impression that he felt sorry for me, and had decided to content himself with the minimum advantage in our match. Overall, the match ended in a score of $20\frac{1}{2}$-$19\frac{1}{2}$ in favour of the Soviet team. I was impressed by Fischer's victory over Petrosian, that of Keres over Ivkov, and Hort's win against Polugayevsky.

Immediately after the match, an impressive lightning tournament was held, with appearance fees for the players, and good prizes. There were twelve players in the tournament, and each had to meet twice. It was held in Montenegro, in the town of Hercegnovi. In view of the strength of the participants, it could well be called an unofficial world lightning championship. The tournament was won by Fischer with the brilliant result of 19 out of 22. Second was Tal, four and a half points behind, and I was third with 14. Then came Petrosian, Reshevsky, Bronstein, Smyslov, Ivkov, Matulović. . . .

Following this came a fairly strong international tournament in Rovinj-Zagreb, which was played under good conditions, especially the first half when the participants lived and played on an island resort, in a quiet hotel. After Fischer's victory over Petrosian in the Rest of the World match (and after all, he had had no practical experience for nearly two years), I was in no doubt that he would win the tournament. That is what happened. I was impressed by Fischer's manner of play. At the beginning of the game, although he has an excellent knowledge of theory, he spends quite some time, as if luring his opponent into a definite, unhurried rate of play, but then in the middle game he readily draws ahead of his opponent on the clock, finding the strongest moves in any position, be it simple or complex. I recall the finish of the tournament. I was fighting for second place, and there was a possibility that I could even catch Fischer, only to do this I had first to beat him, and then to win my two remaining games. In our game I held a slight positional advantage, but on resumption it ended in a draw. After the game, Fischer told me that he had been playing for a draw. This admission surprised me; in a Sicilian he, as usual, developed his bishop at c4, aiming for an attacking position, but no attack resulted, and Black gained a very slightly superior endgame. On the whole, Fischer was very frank with me, and we frequently conversed, discussing chess events, and giving our assessments of chess players.

During this tournament I witnessed an incident which I would never have dreamed could happen. On a free day Fischer was playing his postponed game with Kovačević. Play was held in a hall to which there was an adjoining cafe. Petrosian, his wife and I were sitting in the cafe following the game from a distance. Kovačević, playing Black, had managed to seize the initiative. Fischer, who was defending, set his opponent a clever trap, which I managed to see through. 'How interesting!', I said aloud. 'Fischer is allowing him to win his queen, but if Kovačević takes it, then he may even lose!' Great was my astonishment when Petrosian's wife announced that she was going to tell Kovačević about this trap. And indeed, as Kovačević was walking about waiting for Fischer to move, she went up to him and 'enlightened' him. On the whole, Kovačević played this game extremely well, and had no doubt worked out the complications himself. But it is no accident that, back in Curaçao in 1962, the controllers had reprimanded Petrosian's wife for trying to prompt her husband, by telling him the press centre's opinion of his position. After the draw with Fischer, I lost to Bertok, and as a result shared second place with Gligorić, Smyslov and Hort, two points behind the American.

The 1970 world team championship was held in Siegen. In one of the early rounds I was involved in an unfortunate incident: I overslept before the match with the Spaniards. In fact the first round had begun at four o'clock, and the second was due to start an hour earlier, but I didn't know about this. Being a Saturday, a noisy building site near the hotel was silent. I fell asleep. It should be said that in the Soviet team there are always plenty of free people, who have little to do apart from getting the players ready in time for a match. But on this occasion, they – the team captain and a trainer – rushed into my room an hour and twenty minutes after the start of play, and began telling me off. The game had been scored as nought for us. Incidentally, the team's trainer, Taimanov, would not have had to demonstrate his ability as a sprinter in order to wake me – in Siegen, as in Leningrad, there are taxis, and, as I know from personal experience, it is easier to find a taxi in Siegen than it is in Leningrad. The foreigners later joked that I had not turned up to play as a protest against the Franco regime.

In the Olympiad the Soviet team experienced serious difficulties in their struggle with the Americans. The American team was led by Fischer and played more convincingly than ever before. The deciding role was played by the match between the rival teams, which proceeded most alarmingly for the Soviet players. Geller was hopelessly placed against Lombardy, and Polugayevsky was in difficulties against Evans. Also, Spassky had a dubious position against Fischer, but the Americans were unlucky. Fischer overrated his position, overreached himself, and lost, and the Soviets managed to draw the remaining games. By winning this match, the Soviet team managed to maintain its slight lead, and somehow hung on to first place.

Soon after Siegen I set off for Sochi, to play in an unusual event – grandmasters against young masters. The sports authorities were seriously alarmed about the situation with regard to young players. (In the 1950s, grandmasters had developed one after another. First there appeared the Geller–Petrosian–Taimanov–Averbakh group, and then a few years later the Tal–Spassky–Korchnoi group. Around 1960 there appeared yet a further group Stein–Polugayevsky–Vasyukov. Then, for a whole decade – a complete lull. There were young players, but their standard was not very high, and they were a long way short of the grandmaster title, to say nothing of grandmaster strength.) The amount of attention that was devoted to them! They began holding competitions for children of all ages, and grandmasters were assigned to talented youngsters for coaching; international youth tournaments, special training sessions, matches against adults were all organized, and now even a special tournament – grandmasters against masters. Jumping ahead, it must be admitted that this work was not in vain, and the grandmasters appeared: Karpov, Tukmakov, Kuzmin, Vaganian, Romanishin, Gulko and Tseshkovsky. True, unlike previous generations, this glittering battalion (with the exception of Karpov) is not yet storming the chess heights.

It was interesting to play in this double-round tournament, and to find out just how well these young masters played. But competitively I was not at my best. I lost both games against Kupreychik and Kuzmin, and also lost one to Tukmakov. One very slight consolation was that I won both games against Tseshkovsky. But in the end I did not even score fifty per cent.

* 13 *

A New Trainer

The succession of failures in 1969–70 caused me serious anxiety, for the next World Championship Candidates' cycle was coming up. I sought ways to enliven my rather jaded play, and regain my fighting form. During the summer I played a training match against Bronstein, with an unusual time control: half-an-hour for the first twelve moves, then an hour for the next sixteen, once again an hour for sixteen, and then half-an-hour for the remainder of the game. An original method of training against time trouble! We played six games. Bronstein proved to be the more skilful, and he won with a score of $+3 -1 = 2$. I was dispirited by the result, but, as it later turned out, the match was beneficial to both of us.

In preparation for the forthcoming 38th USSR Championship, I began working with a new trainer. My previous assistant, Furman, who had previously shown his inconstancy on more than one occasion, was now working full-time with the young star, Karpov. It was the young Leningrad master Sosonko who became my trainer. As a practical player he was little known at that time, but he had already demonstrated his capabilities as a trainer. One who spoke highly of his gifts was Tal. Incidentally, Sosonko had helped Tal at the time of the match between us. In the Pioneers' Palace in Leningrad where Sosonko worked, his coaching capability during competitions was legendary. Sosonko had the ability to guess correctly what course the game would take on every board in a team event, and therefore his advice to the lads was extremely valuable. I was not mistaken in my choice of trainer. In the USSR Championship I began without any great sparkle, and lost early on to Tukmakov, but this proved to be my only defeat in the whole tournament. Developing a fast pace during the middle of the tournament, I finished two points ahead of Tukmakov, who took second place. And with the young players I dealt severely: I won against (game 52) Karpov (in this tournament he finished fifth), Vaganian and Podgayets. The part played by my trainer in this success was invaluable.

Early in 1971 I played in the tournament at Wijk aan Zee. After achieving a major success in a particular tournament, there is probably little point in playing there again a short time later. The chances of repeating the success, to say nothing of surpassing it, are slight, whereas a good but nevertheless inferior result will be looked upon as a failure.

On this occasion I did not shine. In the first half I lost a game to Andersson. Before me sat a boy, with his legs somehow unprofessionally tucked underneath him. I was unable to concentrate and play seriously. Then I saw that I stood worse, and offered a draw. The boy was embarrassed, and blushed, but found the strength of mind to decline the offer. I began playing for all I was worth, but it was too late. The young Andersson, after his usual time trouble, avoided all the hidden traps, and won. I had to make up for my negligence towards the finish. By winning several games in a row, before the last round I was half a point ahead of a large group of players, which included Hübner, my opponent to be. This last game (game 53) was of great significance; if I had lost, I would probably have shared seventh place. The game was played in the morning, as is customary in some international tournaments. Hübner gained the advantage with Black, but we made numerous mistakes. It was Hübner who made the last one, and I won.

There is no uniformity in the organization of chess events. There are two types of schedule. The first is to play five hours a day, and to allocate a special day for adjournments after every few rounds. The other form is five hours' play, a short interval, and then an adjournment session for a further two hours. Sometimes a morning adjournment session is also added.

The idea of resuming games the same day, or as soon as possible, is to shorten the game, to reduce the time available for analysis, to avoid the interference of outsiders, and also to cut down the running costs of the event. However, if we consider that a player who adjourns a game works not just from five to seven hours, as is usual, but (including preparations for the game and analysis of the adjourned positions) from eight to twelve hours, then it becomes clear that the trade unions should stand up for him.

It is unpleasant for the players, when the organizers arrange for play to take place in the morning. This upsets the players' accustomed routine for the sake of economizing on a half day's pay. This normally happens in the last round of many events. The games from such last rounds, in view of the large number of mistakes, are not fit for publication!

After the game which I have described, Hübner, a man of principles, resolved never again to play in the morning. And I agree with him. Once – in 1966 at Havana – I lost in a morning game to Calvo in sixteen moves.

As I have mentioned the next Candidates' cycle was approaching. In the first match I was due to meet Geller. The young grandmaster Karpov offered me his services, and we played a training match. This match was completely secret, especially since Karpov was a member of the same Sports Society as Geller. One can understand Karpov: he hoped to gain and, I think, gained a great deal of benefit from a match with me. We played at Karpov's home. I played five games with Black, and one as White. I would probably not have bothered to mention this training match, had it not been for the fact that, shortly before our Candidates' Final Match, Karpov sent to a British master for publication the games which he had won against me in this match. Before each game I told Karpov which opening I was going to play, so that he could prepare for it – at that time opening knowledge was not Karpov's strong point, and I wanted the games to be of full value from start to finish. Karpov led by 2–0 with one game drawn, but then relaxed somewhat, and I levelled the score. One of the games won by Karpov in the match – a French – was excellently played by him.

In my match against Geller, whom I considered an outstanding theory specialist, and a bold fighter, with a fairly subtle positional understanding, I decided to adopt the Sicilian Defence as Black. In the first instance I decided to try the Dragon Variation, hitherto played with success by Sosonko. Geller is quite a good attacker, but he calculates variations badly – he wastes a lot of time, and often does not believe himself. Therefore the risk seemed justified to me. As White, on the other hand, I prepared to do battle against the King's Indian, of which Geller is so fond, and which I find equally pleasant to play against as White. At the same time I prepared an interesting innovation in a well-known variation of the Queen's Gambit, which was quite often adopted by Geller. . . .

In the first game of the match Geller equalized, but got into time trouble where, as is well known, it is not easy to maintain the equilibrium in a position where both sides have chances. As a result he lost. The second game was a tense, nervy struggle. The advantage swayed first one way and then the other, but at the point where Geller had obtained real winning chances, he accepted my offer of a draw. The third game also ended in a draw. In the fourth, as in the second, I played the Dragon Variation. After lengthy consideration, Geller succeeded in improving on the book line. In a sharp middle game he gained a material advantage, and slightly the better chances. We both got into desperate time trouble, in which I blundered on move 37 and lost. This levelled the scores, and it appeared that there was a full-blooded struggle in prospect. But in fact the excitement had overtaxed Geller, and he no longer wanted a sharp tactical struggle, whereas I continued to involve him in one.

In the fifth game (game 54) Geller played not the King's Indian, but the Queen's Gambit, hoping for a draw as quickly as possible. I played my prepared innovation. I personally consider it to be quite an important one, but for some reason it did not even appear in the list of thirty innovations mentioned in the appropriate issue of *Informator*. Geller thought for a long time, but did not succeed in fully resolving the new situation. I put strong pressure on the hanging enemy pawns, and quickly won. In the sixth game, I repulsed Geller's onslaught in the Keres Variation of the Scheveningen Sicilian, though not without difficulty, it's true. Then in the seventh Geller once again turned to the King's Indian. He played the opening imaginatively, and obtained an excellent game. In the middle game I managed to neutralize the pressure on my position, and there was now a slight advantage on my side. The game was adjourned in a position which, 'according to the experts', was better for me. But hard as I tried, I could find no real advantage. I attached great importance to the resumption of this game, and therefore the following day, for the first time in the history of matches for the World Championship, I asked for a postponement on the adjournment day! I prepared to play the eighth game the day after this, but now it was Geller who asked for a postponement. I don't know what he had in mind, but I devoted these days to a serious analysis of the position. There was no possibility of winning by quiet play. My second, Osnos, suggested an unexpected piece sacrifice. It too did not give a win, but Black was forced to defend accurately, and White did not risk a great deal – he could still draw. I don't know what Geller did for those three days, but of course he hadn't analysed the piece sacrifice. At the board he failed to find the best defence, and in addition again ran short of time. I won.

It was now sufficient for me to draw a couple of games, in order to win the match, but I did not change my tactics. I again played the Sicilian. In a Scheveningen Variation my opponent gained a very strong attack, but could not bring it to a successful conclusion. By winning this game too I concluded the match with the convincing score of 5½–2½.

Another of the quarter-final matches, that between Fischer and Taimanov, ended in the sensational result of 6–0. Prior to the match Taimanov had been boasting about how he would beat Fischer. His basic argument was as follows: 'Fischer plays like a machine, and in fact he is essentially a machine. But I am a man! A computer has never yet won against a grandmaster. Therefore I am confident of success.' On several occasions Taimanov made such pronouncements in the press or in lectures. In fairness, it should be noted that, out of caution, the central press did not publish such pronouncements.

Now, after his crushing defeat, Taimanov had to be punished, and punished severely. Normally chess players are not searched when crossing the border, but Taimanov was asked to open his luggage for examination. They found one of Solzhenitsin's books, which Taimanov had brought from Canada.

On the eve of Taimanov's arrival, an international telephone call was intercepted, from which it was discovered that Taimanov was carrying some money from Euwe to be handed over to Flohr. At the customs Taimanov did not declare this money, and was caught red-handed. Yet another crime.

A draft order was published by the Sports Committee, to the effect that, for breaking the rules of conduct for a Soviet citizen travelling abroad, Taimanov was to be stripped of his title 'Honoured Master of Sport', and was to be excluded from the USSR team. This draft was given to all the other grandmasters to read, for their edification, and we all signed it in recognition of having absorbed the lesson.

Meanwhile, time was passing, and Larsen had already managed to lose three games to Fischer! As for Taimanov, he was not really so guilty. When the order was finally published, he remained in the USSR team, and so kept his monthly pay. But, in his native Leningrad, the strict Party authorities took their own measures. Taimanov – a child of fortune, the life and soul of the party, and a pretty fair journalist and commentator – was denied the opportunity to write or make public appearances. He became a *persona non grata*, and was avoided like the plague. The cheerful smile disappeared for a long time from his face. To be shunned in society was unbearable for him. It was then that he decided on a new 'crime'.

After being an excellent family man for twenty-six years, in this dark period of his life, with his political and family ideals collapsing, he left his wife, and married another woman. It should be borne in mind that this must have been especially difficult for him, since his first wife had been the other half of his piano duet, and in leaving her he lost the greater part of his income.

The deserted wife proved to be a woman of spirit, and also pretty mean. She complained about Taimanov's behaviour to the ruling Party Organs in Leningrad. The retribution was not long in coming. Taimanov was finally excluded from the USSR team and his salary as a chess professional was withheld.

This story is characteristic of Soviet life – if we're going to kick a man, then let's all do it together!

I now had to play the crafty Petrosian, whose indifference to noisy playing conditions – Petrosian is deaf – had just driven Hübner out of his wits in their quarter final match in Spain. After falling out with his opponent, and at the same time the controller, Golombek, Hübner had left Seville without playing out the last three games, and thus never received his match appearance fee.

Chess players are of varying character. Some, in order to be confident of success, have to see their opponents as a friend, while others must, without fail, feel enmity towards the opponent, and during a match do not wish to have anything to do with him. The first group includes Spassky, Bronstein and probably Portisch. There are many more of the second type, and it must be admitted that the author himself belongs to this group. In this respect Petrosian occupies a quite exceptional position. He must definitely be on good terms with his opponent, but this is only for appearances' sake, so as to disarm him. In fact, Petrosian is a patent example of the second group of players – but with an extra degree of cunning.

Unfortunately, I was badly prepared psychologically for the match. In the discussions regarding the staging of the match, I was under Petrosian's thumb, and accepted his conditions. From the chess point of view I was prepared 'to the teeth'.

My innovations, prepared for this match against Petrosian, continued to be used up to a year later in international events. I was especially proud, I recall, how in a well-trodden variation, played thousands of times, I managed to think up a new idea as early as the fourth move! My opponent, being lazy, had not bothered with such 'nonsense', and had spent the month regaining his vitality. The match turned out to be highly tedious; we played eight draws in a row! I stood very well in the second game, but played it weakly. I was close to a win in the fourth, but the clever Petrosian managed to save a hopeless position. This was the turning point of the match. In the sixth game, playing White, I just managed to draw, and in the eighth my play again did not come off, and a quick draw was agreed. People joked that neither of us wanted to win the match, and then meet Fischer; others were convinced that the Sports Committee had not yet decided who to put up against Fischer. In the West many were thinking the same way, being unable to believe that the match was being played seriously. And only those who knew me well realized that I was trying very hard, but that my play was not coming off. I was most upset when, in the heat of the moment, I overreached myself, and lost from an excellent position in the ninth game. Never mind, two months later Petrosian too was to have a position to see in his sleep every night! This was the one from which he lost the game which became the turning point in his match with Fischer.

It was not difficult to guess that the last game of our match would finish in a draw, and Petrosian went through to meet Fischer. By his play against Hübner and me, he did not deserve a place in the Final Candidates' Match. But only Fischer was able to demonstrate this.

After winning the match against me, Petrosian persuaded me to take part in his preparations for Fischer. For two weeks I visited his ostentatious villa on the outskirts of Moscow. Before his departure for Buenos Aires, Petrosian insisted that I should also go. The question was debated in the Sports Committee. I said that I was a participant in the same Candidates' cycle, and so it was unethical for me to be a second, but that I could agree if Fischer were to allow me. And I said further that it wasn't always pleasant for me to watch

Petrosian's play, to say nothing of carrying responsibility for it. In the Committee they did not insist, evidently realizing that the devil himself wouldn't help Petrosian against Fischer!

When Petrosian returned, he stated that if I had been there, then he would have won. (That was another thing for me to be pleased about!) In Buenos Aires Petrosian's wife slapped Suetin's face for his poor analysis of the sixth game.

Petrosian was not badly prepared for the match, so what happened? It was obvious that he was very afraid. He does not like, and is unable to play every day, whereas Fischer, like no one else, has the ability to keep his opponent engaged in a constant battle. True, Petrosian did manage to extract one colourless draw out of Fischer, but that was all. Exhausted by having to fight every day, he lost the last four games in a row at the finish.

Petrosian's reaction after the match was interesting. In *64* he reported that at first he had been playing well, but that then something incomprehensible had happened, and he had begun playing badly. On arrival, he complained that they had attempted to roast him in his hotel, and that Fischer had organized an explosion in the hall, so as to play on his nerves. The essence of his speeches and articles was as follows: 'Fischer is the first big-time professional in chess, and, in order to achieve success, he will resort to any means.' He was clearly trying to shift the blame on to someone else. He did this so skilfully, that, unlike Taimanov, he did not suffer at all—due no doubt to his political dexterity.

* 14 *

The Decline Continues

Late in the autumn of 1971, the international Alekhine Memorial Tournament took place in Moscow. It demonstrated that Soviet players were still pretty strong, but at the same time showed the growing degradation of the Soviet School. The tournament victors – Stein and Karpov – won four games each, and drew all the remainder. How peaceable, and what a low percentage result! I received a special prize for the highest number of wins – six – but I also lost six games, and finished outside the prize list. I played quite well in the creative sense, and won several excellent games, against Byrne, Spassky and Tal (games 55–57). Although I was not at my best competitively, I was on the whole happy with my play.

At the end of the year I travelled to a tournament in Hastings with Karpov. I found playing difficult, and was in time trouble in every game. At the start I again lost to Andersson, on this occasion not even daring to offer a draw. Karpov was playing brilliantly, and in the middle of the tournament appeared to have already assured himself of first place. At the point when, towards the finish, he as usual began drawing, I stepped up the pace. My game against him in the penultimate round proved to be decisive. I won this game convincingly (game 58), and before the last round was now half a point ahead of him. I had Black against Najdorf, and he was White against Markland. I did not want to take any risks, and so my game quickly ended in a draw. Karpov adjourned his game in a slightly better ending. I sensed how important it was for me to be the sole winner of the tournament. I remembered Petrosian, and I remembered Suetin, who helped Silvino Garcia to analyse his game against me in the last round of the 1969 Havana tournament. But I decided that what was most important was my reputation. And besides, a young player needs to be educated, even if only indirectly.

So at the time when Karpov was analysing his position, I, on the other side of the wall, deliberately moved about in my room, clearly letting him know that I was not interested in helping him. Karpov won the game, and we shared first place.

In the 1972 USSR Team Championship for cities and republics, I scored 5 points out of 8; the result, and my play itself, were both pretty feeble.

My short match with Matulović, played in the USSR–Yugoslavia match in Ohrid, sticks in my memory. On the whole I used to play indifferently against Matulović. For some reason I found it difficult to get him out of the books. On this occasion I was in a very cordial mood. I remember that I was interested in astrology, and it was predicted that everything would be fine during those few days. As a result I played light-heartedly, and scored only half a point out of two. I was forced to put the pressure on in the two remaining games, which I managed to win. Matulović, however, remained happy with the result.

In the summer I played in the IBM Tournament in Amsterdam. At first my play was uncertain, and I scored one draw after another. In one game, against Malich, I even played the King's Gambit – hoping for a change of fortune. Besides, at that time I was writing, together with my early instructor, Zak, a book for Batsford's: *The King's Gambit*. So I had to try and find out for myself what it was all about! I tried, stood very badly, and with difficulty managed to draw. I improved towards the finish, winning four games in a row. This took me up to second place with 11 points, a point behind Polugayevsky.

At the Olympiad in Skopje I played on second board behind Petrosian. The opposition did not appear to be very strong, but nevertheless for a long time the Soviet team trudged along in third place. Ahead were Hungary and Yugoslavia. We lost the individual match to Hungary; I lost to Bilek, who, as always, played against me with great energy.

With one half of the tournament over, the situation had not changed. With the exception of Karpov and Tal, the members of the Soviet team were playing insipidly. The final result would probably have been equally inglorious, had it not been for a sudden stroke of fortune. The next match, with the Bulgarians, again went badly for us. Petrosian very quickly extracted his draw from Bobotsov, and the other three games were adjourned. Tal looked to be drawing with Radulov, I had a drawn position against Tringov, but Karpov was losing to Padevski. Our analysis went on until three o'clock in the morning. It should be said that there were two working trainers in our team, Furman and Keres, and another person with the grandmaster title, who never took part in any analysis, and who by his appearance and behaviour showed that he was not there for this purpose. That is how he was in Skopje, and he behaved in exactly the same way in Bath, at the European Team Championship. Evidently Antoshin thought that it was not fitting for a KGB informant to soil his hands on this insignificant game. But the analysis went on, although to the exhausted analysts it was clear that however much they searched, it was difficult to squeeze out from these positions more than was merited. But the following morning everything turned out exceptionally well. True, Karpov lost to Padevski, but, in an apparently drawn ending, Tal managed to set Radulov a series of difficult problems, with which the latter was unable to cope. (Here an important part was played by Keres, who was an outstanding analyst.) And a totally unexpected thing happened in my game. The unfortunate Tringov (among present-day players, I can't think of anyone who is so unlucky) had not put his scoresheet in the envelope. To this day I don't know what happened to it: perhaps Tringov found it later at home.

The match was won by a score of 2½ 1½, and, inspired by this good fortune, the Soviet team, under my leadership, on the same day defeated the East German team by 3½–½. I won as Black against Uhlmann (game 59). The difficult psychological moment had been overcome. The USSR team moved up to first place, and maintained this position until the end of the event. But right to the very end the lead was marginal. On the last day we played the Romanians, who of course were weaker than the USSR team, but then we had to win by a big margin. Ciocâltea, whom I played (game 60), complained after the game that I had been thumping the clock terribly hard. I don't recall anything of this, I certainly didn't do it intentionally. I was very nervous, in a superior position for some reason went in for complications, and nearly lost. However Ciocaltea overlooked a tactical stroke, and his position collapsed. With my win the USSR team, finally in the last few minutes of the last round, succeeded in establishing itself in first place.

In 1972 I happened to do some acting, in a professional studio, for a film. This was a film about chess, and was called 'Grossmeister' (Grandmaster). It told of a boy who became a grandmaster, and I played the role of his trainer. The very fact that a film about chess was made was a good thing. But the film itself turned out to be rather poor. It was not by accident that I was praised as being the best actor in the film. After all, I was playing in a professional company, among some really talented actors. It can happen that way; if the script is primitive, then even the actors have no means of expressing themselves. Nevertheless, the film was a success among chess players in the USSR and in Eastern Europe.

My last tournament in this tense year was again in Majorca, in November–December. There was something wrong with me, and I played extremely badly. And on this occasion the tournament was not very strong. By a miracle, once again displaying my competitive qualities, I managed to score ten points out of fifteen, and share first place with Panno and Smejkal. Towards the end I felt terribly tired. I remember my game with Ljubojević. It was a lengthy one, but after one of the adjournment sessions I went back to my room, and established that the position was totally won, and that any move except one would lead to victory. And what should happen but, when play was again resumed, I made this one forbidden move. I did not immediately grasp what had happened, but within a couple of moves I suddenly realized that I had given my opponent the chance to create a drawing fortress, which he had been able to set up only with my help.

* 15 *

Once More in the Game!

The 1973 Interzonal Tournament, an important event in my chess career, was approaching. As if to ascertain once more just how badly I was playing, I decided to take part in the Leningrad Championship. Not since my youth had I played so badly in the Championship of my home town! I lost five full-weight games, and scored only 50%. About four months remained before the start of the Interzonal, and right then, in February, I immediately began preparations.

During these months, my purely chess preparations played a secondary role. I gave up smoking, did not touch a drop of alcohol, and endeavoured to reduce all contacts to a minimum, so as to calm my nerves. Almost every day I ran about a mile, and performed other physical exercises. As for improving the working of my brain, there was no recipe I knew that I didn't try! I did certain Yoga exercises, and – for months – took various medicines to stimulate the working of the brain. I did not go on to a diet, but paid particular attention to a number of substances beneficial to the working of the brain. I utilized the services of a psychologist so as to regulate my sleeping, and in general, to calm me down. I was in no hurry to improve my knowledge of chess theory, since for me this was not the most important thing.

A month before the Interzonal, I played in a short event arranged with the aim of assisting the development of young players, and at the same time of raising still higher the prestige of chess in the country. Three teams from the USSR competed – first, second, and youth teams. I had to play against two opponents whom I usually found difficult – Kuzmin, whose style I had never been able to fathom, and Furman, Karpov's trainer, to whom I now had no intention of disclosing anything. Against Kuzmin I won one game and lost one, while against Furman I lost one game in serious time trouble, and drew the other. Despite this indifferent result, I now felt much more confident at the board.

Prior to the Interzonal I worked a little on theory in collaboration with my long-standing trainer, Osnos (Sosonko had already emigrated to Western Europe), and then the tournament began. The players in the Leningrad Interzonal turned out to be much stronger than those in the Interzonal being played at the same time in Brazil, as well being much younger and more competitive. As a result of the compulsory draw, I played against the other Soviets at the start of the tournament. I was favoured by the draw. For instance, in the first round I played Tukmakov (game 61), who up till then had an overwhelming score in his games with me. He played for a win. He wasn't to know that I was in such devilish form, and that a draw would be a great honour for him. After winning against Taimanov, I drew as Black with Karpov. I was fortunate in a difficult game with Kuzmin, when I managed to save a hopeless situation. When playing Black against Tal, I felt somewhat tired, and when he made one poor move, I felt that he too was in no mood to play, and offered a draw. Nothing came of it! Tal considered my offer to be a sign of weakness, and declined it. But after the first poor move came others. In a now difficult position, Tal timidly offered a draw, but it was too late. And with 4 points out of 5 against the other Soviets, I could face the future with confidence. I was playing strongly. I won against two rivals, Byrne and Larsen, both times in clear-cut fashion (games 62–63), and took the lead, well ahead of all the others. But then came a critical moment. In striving to win every game, I went too far against Rukavina, and lost. Immediately I sensed the closeness of my pursuers – Karpov, Byrne and Smejkal. Fortunately, this did not put me out of my stride. Before the last round I was already assured of a place in the first three.

Karpov, who for a long time had been playing only for one of the qualifying places, received an unexpected present in the penultimate round from Smejkal. In a better position, Smejkal first failed to exploit his winning chances, then lost a pawn, and even managed to lose a drawn adjourned position. Now Karpov and I stood level. On the last day we both had White – he against Torre, and I against Hübner. Of course, I had the stronger opponent, but taking into account the fact that for a long time Karpov had not even been dreaming of first place, I suggested that we should both agree draws on the last day. But it is not in Karpov's character to spurn a chance opportunity – he is a maximalist. In the last round he quickly won, but I was not found wanting, and also won in good style (game 64). I recall how after the game I began apologizing to Hübner, and described the situation to him – how I had absolutely no desire for a hard game that day, but that Karpov had insisted. Such an apology on the part of the winner may sound somewhat ambiguous, and insulting to the loser. Hübner remembered it, and this was the reason for a match being arranged between the two of us at the end of 1973.

Along with the tournaments of 1968, I rate the Leningrad Interzonal as one of the best achievements of my life.

The European Team Championship in Bath followed immediately after the Interzonal. We knew beforehand that we would be staying in double rooms. I was asked with whom I would like to share and answered, 'Stein'. In the morning, when we got on the bus that was to take us to Moscow airport, Stein did not appear. They went off to look for him, and discovered that he had died in his room in the Rossiya Hotel. It was a heart attack, the chess player's occupational disease. Those who think that it is easy to play chess are mistaken. During a game a player lives on his nerves, and at the same time he must be perfectly composed. That's how it was with Stein. On the other hand, during his time away from chess he permitted himself a free and easy life, seeking an outlet for his excitable disposition. What a pity. He had achieved a great deal, but had by no means exhausted his possibilities.

I was suffering from fatigue and did not want to play in the team tournament. In addition, there was an unusual factor, for the first time in many years, no trainers travelled with the team; instead there were four spies (including Antoshin). They carefully watched how we spent our time, interfered with our routine, and talked to us now and then, attempting to collect as much material as possible on the mutual relations between us. I disliked this intensely, and looked for a way to pay back these chaps for their excessive surveillance.

The tournament ended, as usual, in a victory for the Soviet team. Afterwards we gave a few simultaneous displays in England.

When a team returns to Moscow, a meeting is usually arranged with the heads of the USSR Sports Committee. The leader of the group reports on the results and conduct of the participants. Then the authorities say their piece. It is a tedious procedure, that is repeated year after year. The same happened this time. After all kinds of laudatory words, uttered by the various leaders, there finally came the question: 'Does anyone wish to add anything?'. It was here that I 'added' a speech that I had prepared long before. 'Chess players, people who travel all over the world, should be trusted, or else not sent anywhere at all. Why are these four people sent along to supervise us? With their meagre experience, all that they did was interfere, more than ever before. And when they were needed, they weren't to be found. Just imagine, the day before yesterday, I was giving a simultaneous in the City of London, in one of the insurance companies. In the middle of it a man came up and said to me in English: "I don't wish to disturb you, but I would like you to pass this piece of paper on to the Soviet Ambassador in London. Freedom for Soviet Jewish prisoners!" – he shouted in conclusion.' (I beg the forgiveness of this unknown fighter for democratic freedom. I needed this paper in Moscow.) 'And where were those four', I continued, 'who should have been defending me and giving this man an appropriate rebuke?' I said this all very seriously, whereas in point of fact I was mocking them. From the authorities' point of view, the agents had made a mistake, but as far as I was concerned, why was this surveillance necessary? Thank God, none of the four was there, otherwise there would have been a proper scandal! But even so the commotion in the hall was quite considerable. They straightaway took the paper from me, as material proof of what happened. I had spoken out and criticised the authorities. It is not usual to criticise the authorities to their face, especially in the land of so-called 'democratic centralism'. But there was nothing they could do with me. By my play in the Interzonal, I had shown that I was one of the real contenders for the World Championship, and for the moment I had to be endured. Later, when the hour of retribution arrived, I was reminded of this speech.

In the autumn the 41st USSR Championship took place, organized on a new system. With the aim of enlivening the chess life of the country, and also of obtaining the full participation in the tournament of the strongest grandmasters, they began holding two championships – the first league, and the premier league, as they are now called. In the first such premier league they succeeded in attracting all the big names without exception (but the prizes, meanwhile, remained the same as before). I don't recall ever having played in such a strong tournament. The few masters playing were the winners of the first league, and were not far short of grandmaster strength.

The play was very serious, with hardly any tame draws. According to the rules, one half of the participants were to be relegated to the first league. The grandmasters were unhappy about this condition, and wrote a collective letter to the Chairman of the USSR Sports Committee. This was a rare show of unanimity by men who are not united in a common trades union, men who despite their common interests are divided by the specific nature of what is essentially an individual activity. The authorities skilfully exploit their lack of unity and, in cases of necessity (e.g. disobedience) deal with them individually. Thus the grandmasters did not receive a reply to their letter, and everything remained just as it had been thought up by the petty tyrant Baturinsky, head of the chess movement in the country, and a former prosecutor from the Stalin era, now in honourable retirement.

Even to this day the tournament sticks in my memory as a terrible nightmare. One could play a dozen games, and wait in vain for a brief moment of fortune, or battle for victory in every game, and not win. That's what happened to Smyslov, Keres and Tal, who spent the whole tournament in the minus zone. I was fortunate. In the middle of the tournament I managed to win three games in a row, against Rashkovsky, Smyslov (game 65) and Savon! But then, however hard I tried, I was quite unable to improve on this. In the end I shared second place with Karpov, Polugayevsky, Petrosian and Kuzmin. The real hero of the tournament was Spassky. He seized the lead, won several high-quality games, and confidently took first place, a point ahead of the field.

I remember my game with him from one of the last rounds. Interest in the tournament was enormous, the hall was full to capacity, and we were playing, incidentally, in the very same hall where I played my first Championship in 1952. There was no longer that enormous portrait of Stalin in the hall, but technology had advanced, and first-class buildings had appeared in Moscow, built according to the latest achievements in science and technology. But the country is proud of its traditions, and we played in this old hall, sometimes even to the accompaniment of the thumping of a steam hammer, reminding us that it was no longer 1952. With this enormous crowd filling the hall and making an unimaginable din, I, though normally insensitive to noise, realized that I could not go on playing under such conditions, with time trouble approaching. I remembered my acting experience from the cinema, plucked up the courage, and shouted into the roaring hall 'Shut up!'.

In a moment everything was quiet. I made a move which, as it turned out later, lost me my advantage, and I offered a draw. My opponent realized the agitated state I was in, but the position gave him no objective grounds for refusing the draw. After a short think Spassky accepted my offer – and won the tournament.

Spassky's career, which has been nearly as long as mine, has been much fuller than mine in excitement and incident. As a fellow-traveller and a living witness of Spassky's progress, I can testify that I know no man who is more capable of self-perfection than Spassky. As a chess player he has trodden a difficult path. Stumbling and falling, lifting himself up with new strength, he reached the top – the World Championship title. Then with honour, after a struggle, he relinquished his throne to a stronger player. As an individual too he has trodden a steep and tortuous path. After falling under the influence of certain persons, he has outgrown them and freed himself from their oppression. From being an average member of Soviet society – featureless, unreasoning, submissive – he has become an independent, discerning thinker, and has gradually turned into a dissident.

As world champion, Spassky behaved relatively independently from the political point of view. There is a well-known incident when Spassky refused to sign a collective appeal for the release of Angela Davis. He spoke out boldly and independently in lectures. Such lectures were on chess, but in the Soviet Union any topic has political connections. At a lecture in Novosibirsk, Spassky was asked why Keres had never become world champion. He replied before a crowd of many thousands: 'Keres, like his country, has not been favoured by fate.' I should remind the reader that the country in question is Estonia, forcibly annexed by the USSR in 1940.

All this was forgiven as long as he was a famous Russian, the world champion. But then one day he stumbled: he lost the match against Fischer. Then he was reminded of his sins.

The authorities stole up on him gradually. Only in 1975, when even his personal property and his life began to be threatened, did he realize the power of revenge of the Soviet authorities. But his difficulties over travelling abroad began straight after the match with Fischer.

Thus Spassky desperately needed to win this tournament, more than at any time in the past. He played with great energy and will power. He achieved his goal, once again demonstrating his exceptional talent.

* 16 *

Matches with Hübner and Mecking

At the end of the year I succeeded in arranging another interesting event. It rarely happens under Soviet conditions that one can take part in a previously unplanned event at short notice, and this demonstrated my importance at that time to Soviet chess and its authorities. On the proposal of Hübner, a match between us was organized by the West German Club 'Solingen 1868', and took place in Solingen in December 1973. We played a total of eight games. I succeeded in winning the first two. In the first, as Black, I lured my opponent into a set-up unfamiliar to him, and gradually strangled him (game 66). In the second I obtained a slightly better ending. The game was adjourned in a position where Hübner had every chance of a draw, but he did not seal the best move; in addition he analysed the position carelessly, and lost. The third game was won by my opponent. In certain respects this game was critical. I was preparing for the match with Mecking, and I had to find a sound counter for Black against 1 e4. On losing this game, essentially from the opening, I drew the necessary conclusions, and overhauled my opening preparation. The remaining games, where I did rather more of the pressing, ended in draws. Each of us, it would seem, was satisfied with the competitive and creative results of the match. Hübner had shown me, and indeed himself, that he could compete with me; I had managed to test several important opening set-ups, and had once again convinced myself that age in chess is not such a great hindrance.

On returning to the Soviet Union, I had a few days' breathing space before travelling to the USA, to Augusta, Georgia, for the match with Mecking. I had prepared for the match at an earlier stage. There was no need to remind me that my opponent was a strong player: the winner of an Interzonal tournament cannot be otherwise – even though it is less likely that he would have won it if the tournament had not been held in Brazil, on Mecking's home ground. Prior to the match my score against Mecking was 1–1 plus two draws, and if only on account of this I was not reckoning on an easy win. A sentence written by Petrosian in the weekly *64*, following the 1972 San Antonio tournament, struck me as absurd: 'Mecking will never be able to play well, because he does not understand certain elementary things in chess, and never will.' The simple fact of the matter was that Petrosian had already managed to fall out with Mecking too.

On my own initiative, I suggested that a leader be attached to our delegation. My reasoning was as follows: 'In his time Spassky was criticized for having refused to take a leader in his group which went to Reykjavik for the Spassky–Fischer match. Later this was reckoned to be one of the reasons for his defeat: Geller, who was appointed leader, was unable to deal correctly with a series of complex legal problems which arose during the match. Am I sure that I will win this match? No, of course not. Then in the event of failure let a share of the blame fall on my leader!'

So there were four of us who set off for America, the leader of our delegation – a worker in one of the Party Organs in Leningrad, whom I met properly for the first time at the station – my trainer Osnos, and my wife. I will remind the reader that it is not at all easy to take one's wife to an event abroad, but this was something exceptional! In Augusta we were met cordially. The newspapers displayed a lively interest in the match. I was cautious in what I said, and complained of getting old. They wrote about me sympathetically: 'The 42-year-old veteran is experiencing difficulties even before the start of the match.' Mecking too was not particularly talkative, publicity was not so important to him then, and he fully appreciated that I would be no push-over. Although Mecking is regarded as one of the more difficult players, for tournament arbiters to cope with, I can't say that I have anything to complain about regarding his attitude to me. I sensed that Mecking respected me, and wished to behave as well as possible. If occasionally it did not work out this way, I sensed that this was not done on purpose. He was indeed nervous, and was disturbed by the noise in far-off rooms, and once during one of the last few games he indicated to me that he was being disturbed by my heavy breathing! But I couldn't take any offence at him on account of this. He arrived for play in a T-shirt, on which there was written: 'Drink Brazilian Coffee'. This shocked me somewhat, as I am accustomed to turning up for any chess event, especially one with the public present, dressed as for a festive occasion, a performance where I am one of the main actors. This puts me in the correct mood, and the spectators, even if they are not chess players, appreciate the importance of the event. But that is his affair, and it is possible he may come to share my view!

The match turned out very difficult. In the very first game Mecking refuted at the board one of my prepared opening set-ups. A position of approximate equality was reached, but Mecking got into serious time trouble, and, in an effort to strengthen my position, I incorrectly sacrificed a pawn. Mecking took the pawn, coped with his time trouble, and when the game was adjourned I realized that I stood badly. However much I tried, I could not find any way to save the game. However, my second reassured me by pointing out that there were still a number of technical difficulties in Mecking's path, and that, being a young player, he would not be able to analyse the position well. When the game was resumed, although I was in a bad position I played calmly and confidently, as though there was nothing amiss. Mecking's analysis was rather weak, and my confident appearance and the fact that I played easily, practically without thought, confused him. After a series of mistakes by Mecking, I succeeded in saving the game.

The play in this game after the adjournment led Mecking to believe that the game had been analysed for me in Moscow, and that they had told me by telephone how I should play, and he stated this in the press. Now this offended me. After all, such a thing is impossible, and quite absurd. The simple fact was that the class of the analysis by Osnos and me was much higher than that of Mecking and Andersson. But I think that Mecking was later to regret his pronouncement. The first four games ended in draws, but then in the fifth Mecking took the liberty of playing on his birthday. After achieving a good position, he ran short of time, and by bad blunders lost what was first a superior, and then an equal position. On the whole, a chess player is afraid of playing on his birthday, and this is not just a matter of superstition, or even based on the theory of human bio-rhythms, which is quite popular at present. It is just that on this day the player is in festive spirit, but not in the right mood for a game of chess: he is subconsciously unable to get in the right mood for play, for a hard fight.

The sixth game ended in a draw without any particular adventures, and then in the next game battle was renewed. The point was that my main preparations for the match had been made regarding what to play as black, and I was able to equalize fairly accurately, being in principle prepared to draw. On the other hand with White I felt obliged to play for a win. But in his turn, Mecking, in preparing for the match, had analysed, so he said, 1200 of my games, and had also paid particular attention to his preparations for games with Black. As a result I would tend not to gain any advantage, but would not offer a draw, and would not seek any drawing opportunities. Mecking played the openings subtly as Black, but would think for a long time over each move, so that in the second half of the session I was invariably ahead on the clock. This advantage should not be overrated – in time trouble Mecking normally played well – but even so this was a practical chance for me. Nevertheless, it was not this advantage which determined the outcome of the match, but rather my great superiority in the art of analysis. In the seventh game Mecking again outplayed me, and after a mutual – on this occasion – time scramble, the game was adjourned in an ending where I was a pawn down.

I was sure that my position was lost, but my second comforted me, saying that I had quite good counter-chances, and should be able to save the game. Osnos put a great deal of inventiveness into the analysis of this position; at night, while I slept, he found some interesting possibilities of activating my passed pawn, my one counter-chance in the position, and showed me his analysis the next morning. When I went along to the resumption, I felt confident that I could draw. But I could never have imagined what would actually occur on resumption. Mecking had sealed a bad move, after which there was altogether no possibility of his winning (he should have realized this in his analysis). Every move of mine came as a surprise, to him. He thought for a long time, got into time trouble, but stubbornly avoided drawing continuations. At the point where he could now draw only by making the best moves, he had no time to think. The white QRP advanced to the queening square, and Mecking resigned.

It appeared that the match was decided. The winner was the first to score three wins, the maximum number of games being restricted to sixteen. Mecking had cracked, and I only had to win one more. But I just couldn't manage this. I was very close to a win in the eighth game, but with an extra pawn conducted the technical part carelessly. The ninth game was a tense one in which I finally obtained an advantage, but it came down to the ending 'rook and bishop against rook', which Mecking drew by accurate play. The following two games were also drawn, but then in the twelfth Mecking managed, at last, to obtain a considerable advantage from the opening, and he won in good style. Everything was again unclear. There remained possibly four more games, and I held an insignificant lead of one point. At that point I felt extremely tired. Thanks to the family who were looking after us in Augusta, and who were cheerful and ready to help at any moment, I managed to utilize a short break in the match by going off to relax in the open air for four days. It is not clear how correct it is to take such a decision during an event: a player reduces the tension inside him, but within a few days he has once more to play, and is not always able to return to his normal working routine. But I was upset by my defeat, and considered it to be the result of extreme fatigue.

In this altogether nervy match, the 13th game proved to be the most tense and nervy of all (game 67). Mecking, as Black, played for a win. It may have been possible but I did not manage to punish such a treatment of the opening. He gained the advantage, and the storm clouds began gathering over the white position. A critical point was reached, where Mecking had several tempting continuations. Among them was one which, after a forced variation, led to a position with an extra pawn for him. I don't know what Mecking saw at the board – after the game we weren't up to discussing it – but possibly, after a series of unsuccessful attempts in the match to realize the advantage of an extra pawn, he had ceased to believe in his technique, and decided that he must take me 'alive'. After lengthy consideration (during which time I had to sit with a neutral expression on my face, as if my position was not in fact hopeless) of all the possible continuations Mecking chose to try to increase the pressure. This proved inappropriate and I succeeded in equalizing and since my opponent persisted in playing for a win, I seized the initiative, and won with a mating attack. Only an hour earlier, the result of the match had been unclear, and suddenly it was all over. Both Mecking and I were dissatisfied with the result of the match, and we were both justified in being upset. Throughout the match Mecking had outplayed me; the reasons for his defeat were lack of experience against strong opposition, and inadequate technique. To me, on the other hand, it was clear that, with the standard of play that I had just demonstrated, I wouldn't go far.

* 17 *

Face to Face with Petrosian

Now in prospect was a match with Petrosian, who in an excrutiating struggle had beaten Portisch, an opponent whom he had always found difficult. On this occasion he had apparently exerted himself to the limit, which is in principle foreign to him. My match had also not been easy, but I sensed that on this occasion Petrosian was more exhausted than I was. I was well acquainted with his play, with his strengths and weaknesses; the trouble was that his weaknesses happened to coincide with my weaknesses, and his strengths with my strengths. But I reflected that I was stronger than him in a competitive sense, more of a fighter.

I did not repeat my mistake of 1971. I flatly refused to play in Moscow, where I had been drawn to for that previous match. In his estate on the outskirts of Moscow, Petrosian lives like a prince, with all conceivable comforts, whereas I would have had to take refuge in a hotel, with the usual poor Soviet service. On our joint agreement, the match was arranged to be held in Odessa.

The other match being played was between Spassky and Karpov. It was clear to me that at that time Spassky would be unable to win a match against Karpov, especially since Karpov – the rising star – enjoyed universal support, whereas Spassky was now a social misfit, and, in his own words, was forced during the match to adopt 'all-round defence'.

Prior to the matches, Petrosian declared in the press that in his opinion the winner of the Candidates' cycle would be one of the other pair. Such hypocrisy provoked me into protesting, and I declared that the winner of our match would win the Candidates' cycle. My reasons for saying this were purely to do with chess. Both Petrosian and I were superior to Karpov in our understanding, and in particular our experience of the game, and, all other things being equal, should have been able to beat him. In passing, I emphasized that, as regards erudition and knowledge of opening theory, I was superior to Karpov, Petrosian and Spassky taken together! I wasn't far from the truth, but at that time I had no idea what forces I would have to measure my knowledge against in the near future.

It was expected that, on the pattern of my previous match with Petrosian, we would have to battle to the limit of twenty games. But things turned out differently. As was later revealed, Petrosian prepared for the match in collaboration with Karpov. But those openings, good for Karpov, proved not to suit Petrosian's style, since he is not inclined to go in for a fight from the first moves, nor to look from the very start for the best, and sometimes the only moves. The opening in the first game (game 68) came as a surprise to me, but I played calmly, obtained slightly the better chances, and, most important, a fairly clear plan by which to strengthen my position. Petrosian became nervous, made several mistakes, came under an attack, and in the end did not manage to resign in time, and was mated.

During this first game a dispute arose. In recent years Petrosian had acquired the terrible habit of twitching his legs under the table, usually beginning this about an hour before the time control. The playing conditions were good, but play took place in the centre of the stage in an old theatre, on a revolving circle, as I discovered later. While my clock was going and I was thinking over my next move, Petrosian would sit in his place and cause the table to shake all over. 'It's impossible to play like this; shall we sit at separate tables?' I said to him. This was probably a mistake on my part, and I should have directly notified the controller, but we were on friendly terms, and when it was my turn to move I didn't feel inclined to get up and go over to the controller. Petrosian stopped shaking the table, but after the game wrote a statement to the controller about my behaviour. (I found out about this later.)

The second game ended in a draw after a tense, strategic struggle. It finished an hour before the end of the five-hour-session, so that Petrosian did not have time to use his underground (or more precisely, 'undertable') weapon. In the third game (game 69) Petrosian repeated the opening from the first game. This time I was prepared, being familiar not only with the system, but also with the manner in which Petrosian played it. Everything happened within the space of the first fifteen minutes. I sacrificed a pawn, set up strong pressure, then won back the sacrificed material, and by exchanging queens went into an ending where I was now a pawn up. Without difficulty I broke the bemused Petrosian's resistance, and won this game too. Petrosian requested a postponement, so as to come to his senses a little. In the following game he played for a win in his usual style. In an almost symmetrical position, I did not succeed in equalizing, and Petrosian gained a big advantage. We both ran short of time, but here too he proved to be the stronger, and converted his advantage into a win.

During the time scramble I found it difficult to sit at the table. Petrosian was rocking it, and causing it to shake by the rapid twitching of his leg. I went over to the controller to complain, but he merely shrugged his shoulders – what could he do to help? After the game I wrote a statement to the control team, to the effect that, despite repeated requests, Petrosian was continuing to behave in an unsporting manner, and was disturbing my play. At the same time I also pointed out the fact that there was a large group of Armenians in the hall, who were displaying slogans, and shouting out encouragement to Petrosian, and I asked for something to be done about this too.

In the fifth game (game 70) Petrosian changed his opening scheme, but fortunately I was well prepared for this new variation. My second, Tseitlin, had predicted this very opening, and the position after fifteen moves had already been reached on our board the day before the game. I gained a slight positional advantage. An hour before the end of play, with the time scramble approaching, Petrosian sat solidly at the board and, when it was my turn to move, began shaking the table. What was I to do? I had already used up all the accepted ways of curtailing his behaviour. I gained the impression (and at the board, in a highly tense situation, a player senses his opponent much more keenly) that if earlier Petrosian had been shaking the table subconsciously, by habit, he now realized how much this disturbed me, and with the connivance of the controller wanted to utilize his opportunity. 'Stop shaking the table, you're disturbing me', I said to him. Petrosian made out that he hadn't heard what I said. 'We're not in a bazaar' he replied. On seeing the commotion, the controller rushed up. 'Calm down, calm down', he said. Petrosian seated himself more comfortably, and again began shaking the table. What was I to do? I was playing a match for the world championship, and I was in a trap! My clock was going, and Petrosian would not allow me to play. Then I uttered the sacred and at the same time naïve words: 'This is your last chance!' Petrosian caught this (and, perhaps so did some of the spectators). On the other hand, I gained the chance to continue playing, under normal conditions.

The position at that point was not yet won for me, but I played it excellently. I made several subtle moves, and took play into an ending with an extra pawn, and, despite serious time trouble, adjourned the game with a big material advantage.

Petrosian did not turn up for the resumption. Instead, he wrote a statement demanding that the result of the match be annulled (I should remind the reader of the score – 3–1 with one game drawn), and that he should be awarded a win on the grounds that *I* was stopping *him* playing! It was an unusual situation. The match was being held under the auspices of FIDE, and no one, neither Brezhnev nor Euwe, could annul the result, never mind a FIDE congress. Petrosian utilized every possible opportunity. He phoned Euwe, but he was enjoying a safari in Africa. He sent a 290-word telegram to the Central Committee of the USSR Communist Party, the ruling Organ of the Soviet Union, and, in anticipation of a reply, forced me to take a postponement. The matter became an object of investigation by an arbitration committee under the chairmanship of the Mayor of Odessa; from Moscow came the Chairman of the All-Union Controllers' Team, and from Leningrad they also sent an official representative of the Sports Organization to help. A meeting was arranged, to which we were both invited. Petrosian demanded an apology from me. Since, by speaking to my opponent during the game, I had broken one of the letters of the chess code, I said that I was prepared to apologize. 'Apologize?' cried Petrosian, 'but who is going to return my lost points?'

After some thought, he said: 'He spoke to me so loudly that people in the hall also heard; he should also apologize in public!' I was asked whether I was prepared to do this. It wasn't clear to me what was implied, whether I had to repent with a microphone in my hand, or whether to report on my behaviour to a newspaper. I said 'All right, I can apologize in public, but the question arises, to whom do I have to apologize. The fact is that Petrosian's appearances in the Soviet Union are invariably accompanied by demonstrations by persons of Armenian nationality, and what interests me is, what part does Petrosian play in the organization of these mobs.' Petrosian almost choked with rage. 'That's all', he said. 'He has insulted me, he has insulted my people. I won't play against him any more.'

That was indeed all. Petrosian wrote out a new statement, in which he accused me of chauvinism. It is unlikely, in making such a statement, that he remembered one important detail; my wife who, incidentally, was present at the match, is herself Armenian.

I was persuaded to write a letter of apology to Petrosian. Faintheartedly, I agreed – but of course, this had no effect.

While awaiting the decision from the Central Committee, Petrosian lay in hospital, complaining about his kidneys, but refusing to be examined. When a negative reply arrived from Moscow, he came out of hospital and wrote a final statement, to the effect that he was resigning the match on health grounds.

Afterwards, the top sports authorities attempted to reconcile us. The question arose as to whether we could particpate in the same team in the coming Olympiad in Nice, or whether only one of us would play. Petrosian was gloomy, and only in the presence of the committee chairman did he manage to raise a conciliatory smile – just so that he wouldn't be thrown out of the USSR team. It was no longer the Odessa feud that was tormenting him. I had become for ever his sworn enemy, like Spassky and Fischer before me, for having beaten him.

* 18 *

The Final Test

I was now faced with a match against Karpov, who had won fairly easily against Spassky. There was still a long time to go before the match, but already I sensed that Karpov was the favourite, that he was receiving all possible support, and that everything was being arranged to his advantage. Two trainers were sent with the team to the Olympiad at Nice – Karpov's official trainer, Furman, and his other trainer, Geller, with whom he had already been working, although so far in secret. Geller's functions evidently included 'helping' me during the Olypiad, but fortunately I was already in the know. At the last minute, on Karpov's insistence, Polugayevsky was excluded from the team, and replaced by Kuzmin. Karpov, who had won his match against Polugayevsky, from personal experience considered him a weak player, and in general favoured youth.

During the Olympiad Karpov was happy to play White against anyone, but as Black, and against young players in particular, it was I who had to stand in on top board, e.g. against Torre and Timman. I became aware of the situation I was in, but for the moment these were small matters. Worse was to come. I did not want the match to be played in Moscow, and suggested that it be held in some other town, or at least that half of it be played in Leningrad. Unfortunately, Baturinsky succeeded in obtaining my written agreement to it being played in Moscow – simply by adding a further point to a document I had signed!

The question was discussed as to when play should begin in the match. The usual time was 4.30 p.m., but Karpov insisted on five o'clock. I don't know how he argued his case, although in his position it was not essential to find an argument. But I knew what he had in mind. Since I was older, I would find it more difficult playing after the onset of darkness, in the evening. Karpov, on the other hand, has the habit of going to bed very late, and sleeping until one o'clock in the afternoon, so that it is only by five o'clock that he is in a state to play. Karpov's demand drew protests from the press and television, since this would make it more difficult for them to give reports. The question of the playing time was discussed at a meeting of the organizing committee, and a group there supported me with extensive facts on the matter. The only chess player there was Averbakh, the President of the USSR Chess Federation. He had always been very fair in the past, but here he spoke out in Karpov's favour. The suggestion of the young player was accepted. When I learned of Averbakh's decision, I could not keep silent. I had to make some reply, if only in the way of psychological preparation for the match; otherwise, if I had submitted, I would have lost it without a fight. I sent Averbakh a postcard, addressed to the USSR Central Chess Club, and I hope that it was read by many others before it reached the addressee. Since Averbakh is a tall man, I wrote: 'From cowardice to treachery is but one step, but with your attributes you will easily accomplish it. Sail skilfully with the wind and you'll be all right!' I added in conclusion, and signed it in large letters. I had acquired yet another enemy, but no longer cared. From this point I was playing for a break-out.

Karpov had been chosen as the favourite, and it was clear why. He was born in Zlatoust, in the Urals, in the centre of Russia. One hundred per cent Russian, he compared favourably with me, Russian by passport, but Jewish in appearance. He was a typical representative of the working class, the rulers of the country according to the Soviet Constitution, whereas I had spent my life in the cultural centre of Leningrad, and was contrasted to him as a representative of the Intelligentsia. Besides, Karpov was younger and more promising, the future was his, whereas I would not be playing much longer. Karpov was showered with endearments, and he had become a member of the Central Committee of the USSR Communist Youth Organization, the Chairman of which (also born in Zlatoust!) was his friend. Karpov well understood what he represented: he was a symbol, a banner of the Russian people and the working class. He knew how to behave, and he knew what was expected of him.

Despite a certain polish – he after all no longer lived in the provinces – in his clothes and appearance Karpov deliberately retained features which enabled anyone to see in him a simple working lad. Shortly before the match we each replied to identical questions for a popular Soviet newspaper. These questions should have revealed to some extent our intellectual and cultural level. To the question, who is my favourite author, I named the humorist O'Henry, and gave as my favourite film the 1957 Italian film 'Nights of Cabiria'.* Karpov gave his favourite writer as Lermontov (enthusiastically taught in school) and his favourite film 'The Liberation', a multi-episode picture of the 1941–45 war (an ageless theme in Soviet art) which had recently been released. It wasn't, of course, that Karpov was as ill-educated as these answers might suggest, but he was expected to make such replies. He therefore fashioned his image for the millions of Soviet people, and was not embarrassed about appearing primitive.

Several times I stated in the press that Fischer was an outstanding player, and that it would be difficult playing against him. On the eve of the match, one of the major Soviet magazines appeared with a photograph of Karpov on the cover, with the accompanying text: 'I am afraid of no one, and against everyone I play for a win!'

It was known that Karpov's official seconds would be Furman and Geller. I now had to choose my pair. On one occasion I invited grandmaster Bronstein to my house, to help me in my preparations. We did some work for a week, and then I asked him if he would be my official second. 'You know', he said, 'the match will be in Moscow, and I will help you in any case. I run a chess column in one of the major Soviet newspapers [*Izvestia* – ed.], and if I become your official second, then they won't allow me to comment on your match. He returned to Moscow. In the Federation they knew, of course, where he had been. They phoned the editorial office – and Bronstein was forbidden to report on the match. Distressed, he left Moscow, first to rest, and then to play in the USSR Championship. He returned to Moscow only in the middle of November. It turned out that I had involuntarily deprived my friend of both pleasure and remuneration.

I already had one second, the master Osnos, and I didn't want to break with him, since we had worked together for the two previous matches. I had to find someone who was insensitive to public opinion, and to the 'blows of fate' which could result from this

* A remake of this Fellini film was issued in 1969: 'Sweet Charity' (ed.).

opinion. There was no such volunteer among the grandmasters. My choice fell upon the master Dzhindzhikhashvili, a player with an 'indifferent' reputation in the world of officialdom. The very fact of my choice was a new challenge to the Soviet chess world, no less sharp than my letter to the Federation's President, Averbakh. On the other hand, I knew at least that, if the Party should ask him, Dzhindzhikhashvili would not betray me. But all kinds of weapon were to be used against me. I hadn't yet arrived in Moscow before they began telling me that Dzhindzhikhashvili had met Petrosian, was chatting with Grigorian (also Armenian, so who knows whose side he was on). Evidently they very much wanted me not to trust my own seconds, who in any case were not all that strong. In the end they got their way.

By the efforts of the All-Union Chess Federation, a powerful staff was set up to help Karpov. Apart from the main trainers, there were Petrosian, Averbakh, Tal and Botvinnik. Yes, Karpov persuaded even Botvinnik to give him advice. I was told a story of how once Tal and Vaganian arrived back from the Yugoslavia–USSR match. A car from the Communist Youth Organization Central Committee was awaiting them by the airport entrance. 'We're going straight to Karpov,' said the executive, 'he's having trouble against the French Defence.' And they both went.

It is not surprising that for the match with Karpov I was weaker in the opening. After all, I was essentially alone. Spassky, who very much wanted to help me, was in a bad way after his match with Karpov, and could not render me any assistance. Polugayevsky was terribly afraid that they would find out about his actions, and attempted to help me in analysis without getting out of his car. One who made his sympathies for me well known was Smyslov. For this reason, when he returned to Moscow in November after the USSR first league championship, much as he resisted he was immediately sent off to a tournament in Venice – in case he got it into his head to help me.

Grandmasters Suetin, Holmov and Vasyukov spoke out for me, along with a number of masters. Karpov was not liked by people who became more closely associated with him, and, more important, they saw him as the symbol of reaction. But the helpers were in fact with him, and not with me.

Equally significant was the behaviour of the public. We played in Moscow, in the best halls in the country – in the Hall of Columns in

Trade Union House – the same one where once Lenin's body lay in state, and after him Stalin – and in the Chaikovsky Hall, the best concert hall in the Soviet Union. The match was attended in the main by members of the Intelligentsia, who quietly but persistently supported me. But the Communist Youth Organization Central Committee recruited some of its lads to come along. I remember that, when the twenty-second game ended in a draw, the stage was surrounded by a group of Fascist-like toughs, shouting: 'That's it, that's it, smash him, Tolya!'

The trend of the match, its competitive and psychological course, were never revealed in the press. This would have meant touching upon various non-chess factors. And it would have meant explaining the weak play of the two participants, and in particular, that of the winner. I would divide the match into two halves. In the first half, Karpov was on the offensive. He tried very, very hard; he put everything he had got into it. He forced me to fight, trying from the first minute to the last to make me solve complex problems, and aiming to prolong the struggle, by adjourning every game. He had no doubt that I, being the older, would crack up quickly. But what happened was just the opposite; he wore himself out. It should not be forgotten that Karpov has the appearance of a frail youth, and weighs only fifty-two kilograms. During the match he lost four kilograms. He also suffers from low blood pressure, and it is said that towards the end of the match it was down to thirty over sixty. In an amateur boxing match, such an encounter would have been stopped in view of the danger to the health of one of the contestants.

I did have an assistant though, true, he was not a chess player. He himself offered me his help soon after the conclusion of my match with Petrosian. In the past he had been a Master of Sport in boxing, and had then become a specialist in sport psychology. It was as a psychologist that he offered me his assistance. I don't know how useful this was in the match, but in the field of sport he proved to be very good. We engaged in various sports for almost two months before the match, and shortly before it we would run together some four or five kilometres. I am sure that this preparation played its part.

Karpov himself was soon to sense this. In the first eight games the advantage was clearly on Karpov's side. As Black against me, he made a very subtle choice of opening. It should not be forgotten that his chief adviser was Furman, a man with whom I had worked for years and who knew all my weaknesses. This greatly hampered me in the match. On account of the nature of my chess style, I found it difficult to refute one unexpected scheme chosen against me. We played three games with this opening, and despite my prepared analysis, I was forced to give way. For my play as Black I had several prepared schemes, and I did not know which of these would prove the most effective. It occurred to me that I should try out the most dubious of them, the Sicilian Dragon, at the start of the match. And this is what I did in the second game. I ran up against a painstakingly analysed, prepared variation from which, by a direct attack, Karpov won. It was clear that the whole game, from beginning to end, was analysis. This was Karpov's best achievement in the match, but I found it strange that the *Informator* jury should judge it to be the best game of the year. After all, there was no fight, no creativity. The third, fourth and fifth games were, after strong pressure from Karpov, all drawn. In the sixth I again adopted an experimental opening which I prepared all by myself just before the game. Already I did not particularly trust my seconds (Osnos and Dzhindzhikhashvili). But, at home by myself, I had looked into the position insufficiently deeply. The idea was correct, but involved a pawn sacrifice which I wasn't keen on. At home it seemed to me that I could solve the problem while keeping material equality. But at the board I realized that the line I had prepared contained a flaw. In order to overcome my inner resistance, my unwillingness to sacrifice a pawn, I wasted a whole hour at the board! I obtained a promising position, but could still not rid myself of a feeling of mental uncertainty. From an excellent position I lost literally within a few moves. Though few remember this game in the Petroff and practically no one pays it serious attention, I can testify that Karpov really earned his victory at the board.

It was good that I finally settled on the French, a defence which Karpov and I could have analysed together without him ever gaining an advantage. In view of Karpov's lead, it was already dangerous for me to experiment by choosing another opening, especially at a time when I had no confidence in my seconds. You can just imagine them coming up to Osnos, a Party Member, and saying: 'Why have you got yourself associated with that renegade? You should be helping us, it's your Party duty.' It was quite natural that I should have such strange thoughts in such a dismal situation.

My wife was in the press centre, but people were afraid to go up to her, simply to say hello.

Beginning with the ninth game, I sensed that Karpov was finding it difficult to stand the strain. In this game, for the first time in the match, he offered a draw in the middle game. From the tenth game until the end of the match, I held the initiative in my hands. Karpov beat off the attacks in one game after another – for one and a half months he was on the defensive. I must admit that, however accidental my defeats in the second and sixth games were, they were the result of Karpov's intense pressure, and if I had not lost them, then defeat would have awaited me in the third, seventh or eighth game, where I escaped only by a miracle. Now, on the other hand, it was Karpov who was balancing on the edge of the precipice. The tenth, eleventh, thirteenth, fifteenth and seventeenth games – in each of these I had a position which was close to a win. Under normal conditions, an average grandmaster such as Andersson or Vasyukov would have converted them into a win. But it didn't work out for me. Karpov's play became weaker with each new game. He began making obvious mistakes, such as those in the thirteenth and fifteenth games, but I was constantly pressed for time, and was unable to exploit them. I also had the better positions on adjournment, but the quality of my home analysis was markedly inferior to that of the enemy clan. In addition I used up too much energy on such analysis.

Karpov, who had been hoping to exhaust me, was the first to take a postponement. A man of enormous will power, he had already resigned physically. But it so happened that, during this series of games when I was pressing, I did not have any success. Just the opposite – I lost another game! This was the seventeenth. Before the match, amid the atmosphere of general eulogy of Karpov, I had declared, as a means of self-defence, that I would win the match within seventeen games! It was this seventeenth game that proved fatal. I remember that for the first time I played the Catalan Opening. I untypically offered my opponent a pawn sacrifice. Karpov did not bother to hold the pawn, and without thinking made another move. Equally untypical of Karpov, especially without thinking! I recall how at the board I sank deep into thought: who could have betrayed me? It was natural that in my favourite opening I should gain the advantage, but equally clear that in such a state I was unable to play normally! I let slip a big positional advantage, and the game became level. In seeking winning chances, I ran short of time, and then in an equal position I blundered into a simple trap.

Doubts about the outcome of the match had visited me for the first time during the thirteenth game. After the seventeenth I realized that I would not be able to save it, but towards the finish miracles began to occur. Karpov, who was worn out, lost an equal ending in the nineteenth game, and then I won the twenty-first in the very opening. Some of the public were unable to arrive for the game before it was all over. I remember what a hateful glance Karpov threw at me before he resigned (game 71). It was said that after this game he gave up eating. There were just three games remaining, and Karpov's advantage was minimal. What would have happened if there had been, say, another seven games? Perhaps my opponent would have passed away altogether from the strain? Or perhaps he would have found in himself a second or even a third wind? There was no longer any scope for a struggle, I had only one game with the white pieces: everything hinged on this one game. Towards the end of the match I began receiving anonymous letters of the type: 'Just you try beating Karpov, and we'll show you!' No, I was not afraid, this was not reflected in my play, but I sensed that, if I were to level the scores, something might happen to me in the street.

The last three games ended in draws. By a score of 3–2 Karpov gained a memorable victory, which led him in amazing fashion, without any bloodshed, to the title of World Champion.

The last game was transmitted, as incidentally were all the previous ones, on the USSR Central TV Channel. As one friend of mine so aptly put it (and praise to him for not abandoning me during the match, or even after it): 'You chess players have a special mission. Footballers and ice hockey players are needed to make people drink less vodka, but they show you to the public so that they read less Solzhenitsin!' But let us return to the conclusion of the final game, I had to shake Karpov's hand, and then, alone, I left the stage, where lackeys were honouring Karpov. All this was shown direct on TV, but in the recorded version shown in the news, which was transmitted across the whole of the enormous country, the moment when we shook hands was cut out. Why? The match was over, but they had not yet got even with me. People had to be given the idea that I had behaved badly.

During the match, Karpov and I had been engaged in an obscure psychological struggle, the initiator of which was my psychologist friend. From the stage Karpov had immediately discerned him as an enemy, whom he thought was trying to exert influence on him from the hall, to hypnotize him. He requested help, to his assistance was summoned no less a person than one of the best psychologists in the country, working in a centre on the outskirts of Moscow with the Cosmonauts. I would not say that he disturbed me; the task of this Doctor of Sciences was to render harmless my assistant, who by comparison with him was a modest amateur. My psychologist, Z., suggested that I utilize Fischer's experience and try turning up late for the start of the game by five or six minutes. It worked: Karpov was as angry as the devil. But it is not in the character of Karpov to forgive anybody for anything. He also began arriving late, mainly for the adjournment sessions, and here he broke my record. For the adjournment session of the fifteenth game, he arrived thirteen minutes late, just so as to agree to a draw! There were also psychological nuances at the start of the games, when one of us approached the board and shook hands with the other. In life, if I am not mistaken, it is considered that a young person should show respect to an elder. But not in this match. By his behaviour Karpov gave me to understand that he was the favourite, and that he was permitted to do anything he pleased. At the end of the match he no longer stood up when I arrived to shake hands with him.

The chief controller of the match, O'Kelly, also appeared to be under Karpov's thumb. During the fifth game, in a better position for me, I was thinking over my move. Karpov stood up from the board and fixed his eyes on me. He has such a habit. There is a photograph taken during our game from the Interzonal tournament, where Karpov is caught fiercely and wildly devouring me with his eyes when it is my turn to move. So, although unpleasant, the situation was already familiar to me. I asked Karpov a prepared question: 'Did you want to say something to me?' 'No, no', Karpov replied, and walked off. Immediately O'Kelly came up (while I was continuing to think over my move), and said: 'Karpov complains that you are talking to him during the game.' In effect he had turned into an acomplice of Karpov: first Karpov, and then the controller prevented me from thinking about my move. Then during the twentieth game, Karpov made a move and requested that the game be adjourned, and that I should seal my next move. There was still some time left, a minute or more, but O'Kelly submitted to the favourite.

On the eve of the twenty-first game I wrote a complaint about Karpov's provocative behaviour. I did not write it to the controller, since he was a foreigner; how could I, a Soviet man complain to a foreigner? One shouldn't wash one's dirty linen in public. The complaint was to the organizing committee of the match. I wrote about Karpov's lateness in arriving for play, about how he gave the controller advice, and on how he did not stand up when shaking hands with me. This desperate step was a move towards a break – in a situation where the victor was apparently already known. Whether by accident or not, I won the twenty-first game in nineteen moves. But during the match Karpov was not shown the statement. He was only shown it afterwards, when he was terribly angry. During one of his appearances after the match in Leningrad, in his 'own' officers' auditorium (since 1966 Karpov has been a member of the Central Army Sports Club), he confidentially reported that I was punished not for what I said in the press, but for this very statement written during the match.

* 19 *

Punishment

So, there was plenty for which to punish me. For my deviations in the past from correct conduct (remembering if only 1973), for obstinacy, expressed in my letter to the President of the USSR Chess Federation and in my statement about Karpov's behaviour, and finally, for the fact that I had fought, simply fought against Karpov – the people's favourite, and had caused his titled supporters alarm. ('If you only knew *which* people used to phone the press centre to find out how Karpov was doing', one of the journalists told me.)

A pretext was necessary, and one soon appeared.

The closing ceremony took place. There were speeches, they called Karpov a genius. There were special prizes, of which some came my way. The prize for 'The will to win' was of course awarded to Karpov. With one accord, the press broke into praise of Karpov's brilliant victory. The chess press was less loquacious. A few heavy tears of emotion were shed on the pages of *64* by Petrosian and Gufeld.

In his interviews Karpov, as was customary, demonstrated the logical nature of his victory, and his complete confidence in himself over the whole course of the match. They tried not to recall the name of his opponent. Karpov had won brilliantly, he had simply dragged things out a little, but then what reason was there for hurrying! No one asked me for my thoughts, so that when B. Kažić asked me to say a few words for the Yugoslav news agency Tanjug, I agreed with pleasure.

I told Kažić a great deal. He didn't publish everything and what he did publish he toned down. He did not, for instance, mention my statement during the match about Karpov's rude behaviour. The essence of what was printed in the Yugoslav daily *Politika* was as follows: Karpov was no more talented than the grandmasters he had beaten in this cycle. On the other hand, I emphasized his tremendous fighting qualities, and his ability to use all accompanying factors to his own advantage (I would be ready to sign my name to this even now). I further added that I agreed with Fischer's idea, that in such matches draws should not be counted. It would have been interesting to see how Karpov, with difficulty gaining one draw after another and not escaping from bad positions for a month and a half, would have reacted in this case. In our match he could scratch his head, and be content after such a draw: 'Well, thank God, that's one more over, the limit will soon be reached!' But if there had been no limit, then the match would have turned out differently, and Karpov, though pressed to the wall, would have been forced not only to defend.

The interview published in *Politika* on 3 December 1974 got back to the USSR. It was demanded that I should make written explanations to the Sports Committee. I wrote that I was glad that my interview had provided a stimulus for a professional discussion on the creative results of the match.

There was now something to punish me for. My criticism of Karpov was of course, a crime, but was nevertheless an internal matter, whereas my support for Fischer was considered to be an act of treachery.

Anyone could have spoken out against me in the press, since this was an action necessary for the authorities. But in the USSR it is not so easy to find a person who is prepared to do dirty work such as this. It was then that Petrosian, a faithful servant of the authorities, spoke out against me with particular relish. His rejoinder in the *Sovietsky Sport* was entitled: 'Unsporting, grandmaster!' One grandmaster, under cover of the powerful State machine, using the poisoned weapon of half-truth, inflicted a blow on a fellow-grandmaster, thus provoking a torrent of hatred against him on the part of the ill-informed Soviet millions.

Following Petrosian, the USSR Chess Federation also spoke out in condemnation of me. Then came the publication of the so-called 'workers' letters' under the same very bold heading 'Unsporting, Grandmaster', in *Sovietsky Sport*, which branded me and demanded a severe punishment. There were also other letters to the editors, where it was written that the persecution campaign at present arranged strongly recalled the anti-Semitic 'Doctors' affair', fabricated in 1952. But these letters were not published. One such letter was sent by its writer to me at home. He compared Petrosian with Lysenko and Timashuk, grim heroes of the early fifties.

It was a difficult situation. They were also preparing to 'work me over' in the Party line. I gave in to the persuasion of my few remaining friends, and sent a short letter – of 62 words – to *Sovietsky Sport*, saying that I regretted my interview, which had been given in a state of great nervous tension after the match. For the publication of my apology on the pages of his newspaper, the chief editor of *Sovietsky Sport* received a reprimand. They realized just how insincere my 'confession' was.

Towards the end of December I was called to face a committee in Moscow. I didn't go. Following Petrosian's example, I lay in hospital for two weeks.

Nevertheless, I could not avoid the retribution. On 20 January, in response to a new, insistent summons, I arrived in Moscow. In the Sports Committee I was informed that for a year I would be excluded from the USSR team. 'For irregular conduct' was how it was formulated in the order. They informed me that for a year I was forbidden to appear in any international events abroad, and that my monthly salary would be reduced. I returned to Leningrad.

One of my friends has aptly called Leningrad 'the capital of the Soviet provinces'. Once the main city of the Russian Empire, and the foremost cultural centre of the country, Leningrad has faded in the Soviet era. The inhabitants and its authorities are unable to get away from the idea of the city's significance, and constantly attempt to demonstrate this. But the intelligentsia, which in the past made up a greater part of the city's population, was mercilessly exterminated – in 1937, and also before and after. There were several major 'affairs' fabricated by the KGB, a couple of them in the post-war years. Progressive thinking was eliminated, as were the progressive leaders in any post. And in place of those eliminated, a firmer, 'Lenin-like' regime was put in their place. What it came to was that, after a series of purges, Leningrad became the most reactionary city in the country. If from above, in Moscow, they left something unfinished, or did not deal someone the final blow, then in Leningrad this mistake was corrected.

As a well-known popularizer of chess, I was denied the opportunity to write chess articles, or to appear on television. My flat was bugged, and I ceased to receive post from abroad, especially English and Yugoslav magazines. Five copies of a book *The King's*

Gambit, written by me in collaboration with Zak, and published by Batsford's in England, also failed to reach me. Rumours, started by the KGB, began to spread to the effect that I had applied for an exit visa to Israel. As a result things also became difficult for my son at school. True, he was under age, and did not have to answer for the sins of his father, but if he were to leave with his father for Israel, then his class teacher would catch it. So he was picked on for allegedly bad behaviour and poor progress in his studies.

For more than two months I did not make a single appearance – in a city where there was no greater chess authority or speaker than myself. In a city where millions of people knew me and supported me. After several months I began receiving invitations, and in the Party Committee they evidently waved their hands, and said: 'All right, very well . . .'. Sometimes my lectures were attended by specially despatched people. Anonymous letters began arriving at the Party Committee, suggesting that I was saying 'the wrong things' – about Karpov and Fischer, of course. Occasionally I received anonymous letters with a crude anti-Semitic content. I received one letter which was excellently written from the literary point of view. It was sent by 'a worker', and was full of the most varied information: it had a go at Raikin, the artist, and at Spassky. And in conclusion: 'In general, *Für jedes seine*, as was written on the gates of an establishment which flourished not so long ago in Europe. You'd be better over there.' I later sent this letter to the city's Party Authorities, but naturally received no reply to my enquiry. Perhaps I sent it back to where it had come from?

It was an anxious time. A campaign was being held in the press against Fischer and FIDE, vile articles were being fabricated, and signatures collected for them. It was insisted that I should demonstrate my loyalty, by speaking out against Fischer in a separate article. They demanded that I should assist Karpov for his match with Fischer, by making an extensive analysis of Fischer's attributes and deficiencies. I wanted neither to battle against Fischer, nor to help my recent opponent, but I was pressed to do so. They phoned from Moscow. A meeting was arranged in the Leningrad Sports Committee, the sole object of which was to break my resistance, and to extract from me some kind of material approving the general line taken by the USSR Chess Federation. I realized how important the Fischer-Karpov match was for the chess world, and how in the depths of his heart Karpov was hoping to play it. I wrote an article, but not the kind that they wanted from me. In an effort to have it published, I even sent it to Karpov. He showed it to the authorities, but even he was unable to have the article published in the press. Then another letter to FIDE was fabricated, which said that the Russians were being treated badly. They phoned me, and said: 'Will you please sign the letter to FIDE, and most probably we will shortly publish your article on the World Championship Match and Fischer's conditions?' I gave in, and agreed, but my article never appeared in print. In it I demonstrated that the match should have an unlimited number of games, but I suggested that the number of wins should be cut to eight if the match should be arranged under the burning sky of Manila.

My attitude to Karpov may appear contradictory to the reader, especially when taken over a period of several years. But in fact there is no contradiction: personally, despite the tense course of our match, I bear no grudge against Karpov. After all, who in his place would not have tried to exploit a psychological advantage in order to achieve a desirable victory? But against grandmaster Karpov – the symbol of Soviet reaction – I bore, and still bear, a serious grudge. However, Karpov himself is equally contradictory, to those who know him personally, not just from the newspapers.

Being deprived of the possibility of playing abroad, I decided to travel to the international tournament in Tallinn, especially since Keres and Nei persistently invited me there. The Sports Committee forbade me to play even there, and the Estonian players were reprimanded for their irregular conduct. For Keres this was to be the last reprimand of his life. Returning from Canada, from a tournament in which he was forbidden to take part, but where he had decided to play at his own risk and had ended up the winner, he died on the way, in Helsinki. Again it was his heart, the chess player's occupational disease. As a citizen of Estonia, which was forcibly annexed by the USSR, he was unable to accept Soviet customs, and so was favourably distinguished from the majority of his Soviet colleagues by his honesty and adherence to principles.

I received an invitation to a tournament in Yugoslavia, in Zagreb. I was naturally invited to the tournament of very strong grandmasters in Milan. But there could be no question of any such trip.

Soon Karpov began thinking over my situation. No, he is not a philanthropist, but, on becoming World Champion, he had thought: 'But where is the merit in it?' He had obtained his title for having defeated Spassky and myself. But the people had begun to forget about us: neither Spassky nor I, being oppressed by the State machine, could show our strength. Even to mention one of our names in an article gave it a bad tone! It looked as if he had beaten second-rate players, and that he had obtained his title cheaply. He took certain steps to make things easier for me. Here, a part was also played by the fact that Petrosian had done everything possible to bury the match between Fischer and Karpov, and Karpov, realizing this, was already seeking an ally for his battle with Petrosian. In September I was informed officially that I was no longer in disgrace, that my salary would be resumed, and that I could travel to a tournament in the Philippines, for which the USSR Chess Federation had recommended me. It was here that the Leningrad Party Organization played its part. In order to travel abroad, one has to obtain permission from the Party Organization of one's town, and this I did not receive. Still hoping, I travelled to Moscow, ready to set off to Manila at any moment. Polugayevsky went off, and in the central newspaper *Pravda* a report appeared to the effect that in the first round of the tournament in the Philippines I had played Larsen. In fact I had met Spassky on the day of his wedding to a French citizen, and had congratulated him on his achievement (it is said that the French Ambassador had requested permission in a private audience with Brezhnev)!

In November I at last received permission to play in an international tournament, even if only in Moscow. There was a strong entry, the group of Soviet grandmasters being particularly strong. The tournament was going badly for me, but then came the encounter with Petrosian (game 72), which I played gritting my teeth. It was adjourned with an advantage to me, and I was helped in my analysis by Spassky. During the second adjournment session I won. This encounter mobilized me. By scoring $4\frac{1}{2}$ out of 5 at the finish, I shared third place behind Geller and Spassky, which after a year of anxiety was not at all bad.

* 20 *

The Break

My misfortunes and the filthy accusations, to which I had no opportunity of replying, provoked in me a change of heart. The necessity of sometimes having to submit merely embittered me. Although I was a person of fairly free convictions, I had always been pretty conservative. I had spent my whole life in one and the same town. I was married only once, and I preferred to work with one and the same trainer.

But in December 1974 I realized that, with my obstinate nature, I would be unable to avoid radical changes. Strong pressure was being brought to bear on me, but there was also the feeling that they were awaiting for an appropriate moment, when I should begin playing less strongly, to bring me down completely.

I considered which would be the best method to chose, so that it shouldn't be too difficult, or painful. Submit an application for an exit visa to Israel? This would be like ascending to Golgotha! Once I even wrote a letter (but did not send it) to Tito, asking that he should take me under his wing: it would certainly be better there than in the USSR. But I realized that such an idea was a pipe dream.

But for the moment, in anticipation of the next World Championship cycle, I was sent abroad. At the end of 1975 I went off to the tournament in Hastings.

I had of course hinted to my wife and to my few remaining friends that I could no longer live under Soviet conditions. But neither my friends, nor my wife, could understand me completely: all the unpleasantness touched directly on me, but on those close to me fell a feeling of bitterness and disgrace on my account. The one who was most upset on account of me was my son. During my darkest days he went to school wearing a badge from the Olympiad in Siegen – with *Kortschnoi* pinned to his lapel.

When I set off for Hastings, I took with me a number of chess books and photo-albums. All this I sent after the tournament to Sosonko, now a Dutch master, in Amsterdam. I played badly in the tournament, and took fourth place.

My position in the Soviet Union had apparently begun to stabilize, but I no longer wanted to re-establish old connections. I myself no longer phoned people who had ceased to phone me during my difficult times. Soviet chess publications were expecting material from me, but I didn't write for them. One of the chess journalists had decided to compile a book of games by Soviet grandmasters, and begged me for some material towards it. I refused point-blank, saying that I did not want to spoil his book. Another journalist wanted to write my biography. I delayed matters, and we didn't even meet. And I gave him to understand that in the USSR he would earn no esteem from such a book.

The Federation chiefs enquired several times about whom I intended working with in preparation for the Candidates' Matches. I gave no reply, explaining that since I had been outlawed by the Sports Committee, masters and grandmasters were afraid to work officially with me. That's the way it was, but also I didn't want to put anyone under threat from the authorities in the event of my leaving. During 1975 and 1976 I several times organized semi-secret training sessions with masters who were, in my opinion, good people. It was this that was the chief criterion in my choice of trainer. I also took part in one official training session. For the purpose of helping young players, I went for two weeks to Lvov, where I did some quite useful work with the local grandmasters and masters, to the benefit of both them and myself.

In April came the Team Championship of USSR Sports Societies in Tbilisi. There were few who wanted to play against me. Bronstein didn't wish to, Tal went off prematurely, and Karpov claimed illness, although he was walking about in perfect health that day. The result was that I defeated several reserves, and took first place on my board. In my team I was captain, trainer and leader. It is not surprising that many kindly words were written about me in the July issue of the magazine *Shakhmaty v SSSR*. At the time when the magazine was issued, I was already far away. Doubtless many subscribers failed to receive that issue. . . .

In July I played in the IBM Tournament in Amsterdam. As usual in recent times, I found it hard going, was often in time trouble, and with difficulty shared first place with Miles.

Even then I was firmly convinced that it was now that I should stay behind in the West. I had decided to break with the Soviet Union, but for the moment, with the approach of the Candidates' Matches, the authorities were still interested in me, and I could still travel and collect as many valuables as possible – in the West. I sent my archives off to Amsterdam, particularly precious letters from friends, and no less memorable ones from my enemies.

But I was no longer able to keep silent. A week before the end of the tournament I gave an interview to a correspondent of the 'France Presse' agency. I talked about the reasons for Spassky's poor play in the Interzonal Tournament. At his request I had worked with him for two weeks in Sochi, and during this time he twice had to fly up to Moscow – they didn't want to sign the documents for his visa to Manila. I also remarked that I considered it disgraceful that the USSR should refuse to play in the Olympiad in Israel. (Later, on another occasion, I said that I considered the refusal to be a continuation of the traditional policy of the Russian-Soviet State, the policy of anti-Semitism.) When I saw the interview in print, I realized that a return to the USSR would threaten me with fresh incalculable misfortunes. In giving this interview, I had used my right of being a free man; from this time, although I had never essentially bothered with politics, I had become a 'dissident', and an open one. While I had been in the Soviet Union, I had utilized all legal possibilities to show the Soviet people, using chess as an example, what was really going on in our country – how it appeared in the press, and how it was in reality. From now on, if I were in the Soviet Union, there was no way I could be of use to people. With a clear conscience I took the decision – to remain in the West, now and for ever.

On the last official day of my stay in Holland, I should have appeared in the USSR Embassy in the Hague with a report on the recently concluded tournament, at seven o'clock in the evening.

But at half past five I finished a simultaneous display in the Hague, and went off to friends in Amsterdam. The following day, in a police station in Amsterdam, I asked for political asylum in Holland.

I am not the first, and will not be the last, to seek a release from the far from creative atmosphere inside the Soviet Union, and to resort to running away. But in the Soviet Union I enjoyed a degree of perfectly official popularity that neither Solzhenitsin nor Sakharov could boast of, nor even Rostropovich or Barshai, public figures who are much better known in the West than I am. I was seen on the television screen by tens of millions of people, I was greeted, and my speeches listened to, by hundreds of thousands. For dozens of years the papers talked about me – Stalin, Malenkov, Krushchev and Brezhnev gave way one to another, but my name did not dissapear from the press. I myself sensed this popularity, and it made life easier. This popularity was now turned against the Soviet authorities. The people had to be informed of my disappearance. A sailor leaving his ship, a writer staying behind in the West, a political figure deported from the country – there is no need to report all these. But the incident involving me was impossible to conceal from the people.

First of all, a few days after the incident, Tass reported it. The communiqué was for publication in the West, and was not printed in the Soviet papers. The essence of the report was that all of which I was complaining was untrue, and that it was entirely due to my wounded pride and vanity. It was a stupid report, lacking in logic and causality of events, and it would be silly to bother refuting it.

After twenty days the USSR Chess Federation made an official announcement, and a further two weeks later a letter by the grandmaster members of the USSR Chess Organization was fabricated. After mentioning in passing the treachery to my mother-country (as was once aptly remarked, when a mother loses her human qualities, leads a depraved life, and drinks, she is often deprived of her maternal rights), the 'signatories' laid particular emphasis in the letter on something else. It was that I was unable to conduct myself properly at the chess board, and therefore must be excluded from all events, and in particular from the list of participants in the Candidates' Matches for the World Championship! It was painful to read the names of those who had signed the letter. For twenty years I had exchanged ideas with each one of them, and we had shared our last bread-and-butter. However, I have eye-witness evidence to prove that at least one of them never actually saw the letter, and didn't know anything about it, but that his signature nevertheless appeared below the document. In particular, it should be noted that this crude attack by the Soviet authorities was not supported by Karpov.

On reading the letter, I was once more convinced that I had acted correctly. How my subsequent life will turn out, what will happen with my chess career, I do not know. But I could no longer live under a regime which deprives people of their self-respect.

POSTSCRIPT

The life of a chess professional in the West is a difficult one. Despite the fact that there is now a demand for chess specialists – from my own experience I know that tens of thousands of people in Holland, the USA, Switzerland, Germany and Spain are interested in chess – chess is simply not recognised as a professional sport. In my current passport in the 'profession' column I have put 'Chess Grand Master'. Respectable people read the entry and say 'um, um'. It all sounds very nice, but what, they want to know, was your *real* profession before that? It has always been difficult for professionals to be recognised. Their knowledge and learning seems to have no place outside of the schoolroom. Their skills are not regarded seriously: they are looked upon as mere jugglers. They have neither pupils nor followers. Throughout the entire, fairly extensive free world only a handful of professional grandmasters achieve real status.

The time will probably come when chess will attract the attention of sociologists: in the fight against a rising crime rate we should be replacing television sets with chess boards. In this connexion, as it has been noticed, chess has one big failing: it is not a spectacle and does not lend itself to commercialisation.

In Holland I have been most cordially received – with that hospitality and consideration so characteristic of this small country. The development of chess here has been extraordinary; there are several dozens of clubs, a dozen or so quality players, a few powerful sponsors, including organisations and commercial concerns patronising chess. I quickly signed a year's contract with a firm producing computers – Folmak – who are joint-promoters of chess. I shall be working for them, as a trainer and taking part in competitions as a member of the 'Folmak Rotterdam' team.

My first year in the West has been a difficult, tense one. I was in great demand: interviews alternated with sessions of simultaneous games. Then for two weeks I was a trainer for the Dutch Olympic Tournament. Then more appearances, followed by a training match with Timman. Then in November I found out that I had to play a Candidates match with Petrosian.

As things were at the moment, it seemed that I had no chances in a match against a person so hateful to me. Weighed down with work, having no permanent abode, cut off from my family, I had to stand up to this grandmaster, fattened up and ready for the kill. He turned up in Italy with his wife and a whole troop of grandmasters as attendants.

It was quite difficult for me to find assistance. After all, who wants to help a notorious failure? In the end, I did succeed in locating people – not particularly strong players, but nevertheless exceptionally dedicated. I am very indebted to Hans Ree and Jacob Murei for their valued support throughout this match.

It was an agonising experience and in the newspapers they called it the 'match of hate'. We did not speak to each other, did not shake each other's hand, did not allow our gaze to cross. Through the adjudicator, Kazić, a draw was offered. It struck me that all those people, with whom I was always in contact in the USSR and who had now come to Il Ciocco, were nothing more than a primitive expedition despatched to suppress a fugitive convict. It was as well that the chessboard was the only battlefield. My nerves were, however, somewhat stronger. The standard of play was awfully low. If you had given the games to a computer for appraisal, without naming the protagonists, it would have put the level of play at no more than 2300. In the difficult circumstances mistake came after mistake.

The result of the match was 2:1 in my favour with 9 draws. This shows just how agitated the opponents were. As I left Il Ciocco, I gave Petrosian a last farewell look. He was a whole range of emotions: rage, hate and 'I didn't finish you off today, but we'll settle things next time'. In fact, just after he arrived in the USSR, Petrosian was removed from his post as chief editor of *64*.

It is obvious that this is now my fate to struggle with the USSR, making things for them as unpleasant as I can. The match between Mecking and Polugayevsky was an equal fight, but finished up in favour of the Soviet player $+1 = 11$.

For the last twenty years I had been on friendly terms with Polugayevsky, but nowadays, when his signature appears on a letter, concocted by the Soviet Chess Federation, I haven't had any particular desire to see him and play with him. It is clear that my opponent felt the same thing. I was, by the way, ready to do battle following the preceding match, but for this occasion I could in no way feel relaxed. I even asked if I might greet my partner with a handshake and shortly after that, when the leader of the Baturinsky delegation succeeded in contacting Moscow, I received an answer in the affirmative. Recently I have managed to strengthen my team of assistants. On this occasion I have been helped by two people from England – Raymond Keene and Michael Stean, as well as Murei. I have scarcely played better than in the last few months, and in the gap between matches I won the Dutch championship with good results – 12 out of 13. This put a great deal of confidence in me. It goes without saying that the semi-final went no more easily for me than the match with Petrosian. I won the first three games after which the result of the match was clear. The final score: $+5 = 7 - 1$ in my favour. Recently, on the eve of the match with the 'one-legged dissident' Spassky, I went to live and work in West Germany. It seems I am now exposed to something experienced by Soviet émigrés – the cosmopolitan and free nature of living to be enjoyed in one's new surroundings.

Games

1 Taimanov–Korchnoi
Leningrad Ch. 1950

1 d4 e6 2 g3 f5 3 ♗g2 ♘f6 4 ♘f3
♗e7 5 0–0 0–0 6 c4 d6 7 ♘c3 ♕e8
8 ♕c2 ♕h5 9 b3 ♘c6 10 ♗b2 ♗d7
11 a3 ♖ae8 12 d5 ♘d8 13 ♘d4 e5
14 ♘db5 ♘f7 15 ♘×c7 ♖c8 16
♘e6 ♗×e6 17 de ♘g5 18 ♘d5
♘×d5 19 ♗×d5 f4 20 f3 fg 21 hg
♕h3 22 ♔f2

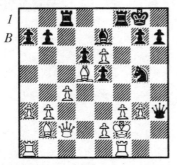

22 ... ♘×f3 23 ♔e3 ♘d4 24 ♕d1
♕×g3+ 25 ♖f3 ♘×f3 26 ef b5 27
♕h1 bc 28 bc ♖b8 29 ♗c3 ♖b3 30
♔d3 ♕f2 31 ♕e1 e4+ 32 ♗×e4
♖×f3+ 33 ♗×f3 ♕×f3+ 34 ♔c2
♖×c3+ 35 ♔b2 ♖b3+ 0–1

2 Korchnoi–Smyslov
½–final, 19th USSR Ch. 1951

1 e4 e5 2 ♘f3 ♘c6 3 ♗c4 ♗e7 4 d4
d6 5 d5 ♘b8 6 ♗d3 ♘f6 7 h3 c6 8
c4 b5 9 ♘c3 b4 10 ♘e2 0–0 11 ♗e3
cd 12 cd ♘fd7 13 g4 ♘a6 14 ♘g3
♘ac5 15 ♗e2 ♖e8 16 0–0 ♕a5 17
♘d2 ♕d8 18 a3 ♖b8 19 ab ♖×b4
20 ♖×a7 ♖×b2 21 ♘c4 ♖b7 22
♖a3 ♕c7 23 ♕c2 ♘f8 24 ♖c3
♗d7 25 ♘×d6 ♗×d6 26 ♗×c5
♗×c5 27 ♖×c5 ♕b6 28 ♖c1 ♖a8
29 ♖c7 ♖×c7 30 ♕×c7 ♕h6 31
♖b1 ♕×h3 32 g5 h6 33 gh ♕×h6
34 ♕×e5 ♖e8 35 ♕h5 ♕f4 36 ♕f3
♕g5 37 ♕h5 ♕f4 38 ♕f3 ♕g5 39
♖b7 ♘g6 40 ♕h5 ♕c1+ 41 ♔h2
♘e5 42 ♗d1 g6 43 ♕e2 ♔g7 44 f3
♕f4 45 ♔g2 ♖h8 46 ♕f2

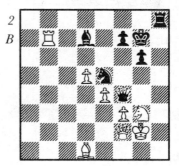

46 ... ♖h2+ 47 ♔×h2 ♘g4+ 48
♔g2 ♘×f2 49 ♔×f2 ♕d2+ 50
♗e2 ♗h3 51 ♖b3 ♕d4+ 52 ♔e1
♕g1+ 53 ♘f1 g5 54 ♖d3 ♗×f1 55

♗×f1 ♕g3+ 56 ♔e2 ♕d6 57 ♔e3
♔f6 58 ♔f2 ♔e5 59 ♔g3 ♔f6+ 60
♔g2 ½–½

3 Smyslov–Korchnoi
20th USSR Ch. 1952

1 ♘f3 c5 2 c4 ♘f6 3 d4 cd 4 ♘×d4
g6 5 ♘c3 d5 6 ♗g5 dc 7 e3 ♗g7 8
♗×c4 0–0 9 0–0 a6 10 ♕b3 ♘bd7
11 a4 ♕a5 12 ♗h4 ♘b6 13 ♗e2 e5
14 ♘c2 ♗e6 15 ♕b4 ♕×b4 16
♘×b4 ♖ac8 17 ♖fc1 a5 18 ♘d3
♘fd5 19 ♘×d5 ♗×d5 20 ♗e7
♖×c1+ 21 ♖×c1 ♖e8 22 ♗a3
♘×a4 23 ♗d1 ♘b6 24 ♖c5 ♖d8
25 f3 ♗f8 26 ♖c1 ♗×a3 27 ba

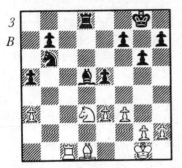

3
B

27 ... ♗×f3 28 ♗×f3 ♖×d3 29
♖b1 ♘c4 30 ♖×b7 ♘×e3 31 a4
♖d4 32 ♗c6 ♘g4 33 ♖b1 e4 34 h3
♘e5 35 ♗b5 f5 36 ♖c1 f4 37 ♖c5
♖d1+ 38 ♔f2 ♘d3– 39 ♗×d3
♖×d3 40 ♖×a5 ♖d2+ 41 ♔f1
♔f7 42 ♖a7+ ♔f6 43 ♖×h7 e3 44
♖h8 ♖d1+ 45 ♔e2 ♖g1 46 a5
♖×g2+ 47 ♔f3 ♖f2+ 48 ♔g4
♔e7 49 ♖h7+ ♔d6 50 ♖h8 e2 51
♖e8 ♔c6 0–1

4 Korchnoi–Botvinnik
20th USSR Ch. 1952

1 c4 ♘f6 2 g3 c6 3 ♗g2 d5 4 ♕c2 e5

5 d3 h6 6 ♘f3 ♗d6 7 0–0 0–0 8 e4
de 9 de c5 10 ♘c3 ♘c6 11 ♗e3
♘d4 12 ♗×d4 cd 13 ♘b5 ♗b8 14
♘e1 ♗d7 15 ♘a3 h5 16 ♘d3 h4
17 c5 ♕e7 18 ♘c4 hg 19 hg ♗c7 20
b4 b5 21 ♘d2 ♗c6 22 ♖ae1 g6 23
♘b3 ♔g7 24 f4 ♗g4 25 fe ♖ad8 26
♕b2 ♘×e5 27 ♘f4 ♘c4 28 ♕f2
♗e5 29 ♘e2 ♕d7 30 ♘f4 ♕g4 31
♕f3 ♕g5 32 ♖f2 ♘e3 33 ♗h3
♖de8 34 ♘a5 ♗×f4 35 ♕×f4
♕×f4 36 gf ♗×e4 37 ♖d2

4
B

37 ... ♗f5 38 ♗×f5 ♘×f5 39
♖×e8 ♖×e8 40 ♘c6 ♖e1+ 41
♔f2 ♖e4 42 ♘×a7 ♖×f4+ ½–½

5 Nezhmetdinov–Korchnoi
Bucharest 1954

1 e4 c5 2 ♘f3 ♘c6 3 d4 cd 4 ♘×d4
♘f6 5 ♘c3 d6 6 ♗g5 e6 7 ♕d2 a6 8
0–0–0 ♗d7 9 f4 ♗e7 10 ♘f3 b5 11
♗×f6 gf 12 f5 ♕a5 13 ♔b1 ♘e5 14
♗d3 ♘c4 15 ♗×c4 bc 16 ♖he1
♖b8 17 ♘e2 ♕b5 18 c3 c5 19 ♘g3
♖g8 20 ♖e2 ♗c6 21 ♔a1 ♕a5 22
♕h6 ♕b6 23 ♕×h7 ♖g4 24
♕h8+ ♔d7 25 ♕h5 ♖×g3 26 hg
♗×e4 27 ♕×f7 ♗d3 28 ♕e6+
♔d8 29 ♖ed2 ♕c5 30 ♖h1 d5 31
♖h7 ♕d6(*5*)

32 ♖×e7? ♕×e7 33 ♕×d5+
♔c7 34 g4 ♖b5 35 ♕a8 ♕c5 36 b4

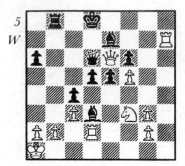

5
W

♕c6 37 ♕a7+ 🖫b7 38 ♕e3 a5 39
g5 ab 40 cb 🖫×b4 41 ♕a7+ ♔c8
42 🖫d1 🖫a4 ½-½

6 Matanović–Korchnoi
Students' Olympiad, Uppsala 1956

1 e4 e6 2 d4 d5 3 ♘c3 ♗b4 4 e5 b6
5 ♕g4 ♗f8 6 ♘f3 ♕d7 7 a3 ♗a6 8
♗×a6 ♘×a6 9 0–0 ♘e7 10 ♘e2
♘b8 11 ♗g5 ♘bc6 12 b3 ♘f5 13
♘g3 h6 14 ♗d2 g6 15 ♕f4 ♗e7 16
🖫fd1 g5 17 ♕g4 ♘×g3 18 ♕×g3
0–0–0 19 ♗b4 f5 20 ef ♗×f6 21
🖫ac1 h5 22 c4 g4 23 ♘e5 ♗×e5 24
de d4 25 ♕f4 a5 26 ♗d2 ♕h7 27
🖫e1 🖫hf8 28 ♕g3 d3 29 c5 b5 30
♕e3 🖫d5 31 ♗c3 b4 32 ab ab 33
♗d2 ♕f5 34 🖫f1 🖫×e5 35 ♕h6
♔b7 36 🖫c4 ♕f7 37 ♗×b4 🖫e2
38 ♗d2 e5 39 ♗e3 d2 40 🖫a4
40 ... 🖫×f2 0–1

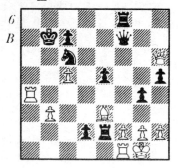

6
B

7 Korchnoi–Taimanov
Hastings 1955–56

1 e4 c5 2 ♘f3 ♘c6 3 d4 cd 4 ♘×d4
♘f6 5 ♘c3 d6 6 ♗g5 e6 7 ♕d2 a6 8
0–0–0 ♗d7 9 f4 🖫c8 10 ♘f3 ♕a5
11 ♔b1 b5 12 ♗d3 ♘b4 13 🖫he1
♘×d3 14 ♕×d3 b4

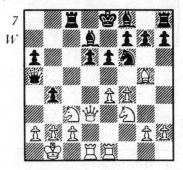

7
W

15 ♘d5 ed 16 ed+ ♔d8 17 ♗×f6+
gf 18 ♕d4 ♔c7 19 ♕a7+ ♔d8 20
♕d4 ♔c7 21 ♕a7+ ½-½

8 Korchnoi–Tolush
23rd USSR Ch. 1956

1 d4 ♘f6 2 ♘f3 g6 3 g3 ♗g7 4 ♗g2
0–0 5 c4 d6 6 0–0 ♘c6 7 ♘c3 ♗f5 8
d5 ♘a5 9 ♘d4 ♗d7 10 b3 c5 11 dc
bc 12 ♗b2 🖫b8 13 🖫b1 a6 14 ♘c2
♕c8 15 e4 ♗h3 16 🖫e1 ♗×g2 17
♔×g2 ♘g4 18 h3 ♘e5 19 ♗a1
♕b7 20 f4 ♘d7 21 ♕f3 🖫be8 22
g4 c5 23 ♘d5 ♗×a1 24 🖫×a1
♘c6 25 🖫ad1 a5 26 h4 a4 27 h5 ab
28 ab 🖫b8 29 🖫b1 🖫fe8 30 🖫h1
🖫a8 31 🖫b2 🖫a7 32 hg fg 33 ♕h3
♘f8 34 ♕h6 🖫ea8 35 f5 ♘e5 36 fg
♘e×g6 37 🖫f1 🖫a2 38 🖫×a2
🖫×a2 39 🖫f2 ♘e6 40 ♔g1 ♘ef8
41 ♕e3 🖫b2 42 ♕f3 🖫b1+ 43
♔h2 e6 44 ♘f6+ ♔h8 45 ♘h5
♕e7 46 ♘f4 ♘e5 47 ♕h3 ♕g7(8)
48 ♘h5 ♘×g4+ 49 ♕×g4

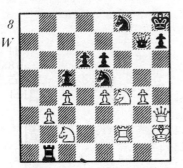

8
W

♕×g4 50 ♖×f8+ ♕g8 51 ♖×g8+
♔×g8 52 ♘a3 ♖b2+ 53 ♔g1 ♔f7
54 ♘b5 ♔e7 55 ♘f4 ♖×b3 56
♘c7 ♖b4 57 ♘c×e6 ♖×c4 58
♘g5 ♔f6 59 ♘×h7+ ♔e5 60 ♘g2
♔×e1 61 ♘g5+ ♔d3 62 ♔f2
♖c2+ 63 ♔f3 ♖a2 64 ♘f4+ ♔c4
65 ♘f7 ♖d2 66 ♔e3 ♔c3 67 ♘g5
d5 68 ♘f3 d4+ 69 ♔e4 ♖d1 70
♘e6 ♔b4 71 ♘e×d4 cd 72 ♘×d4
♔c4 73 ♘f3 ♖d8 74 ♘e5+ ½–½

9 Korchnoi–Spassky
23rd USSR Ch. 1956

1 d4 ♘f6 2 ♘f3 g6 3 g3 ♗g7 4 ♗g2
0–0 5 b3 d6 6 ♗b2 e5 7 de ♘g4 8
0–0 ♘×e5 9 ♘×e5 de 10 ♘c3 ♘d7
11 ♕d2 ♘f6 12 ♕×d8 ♖×d8 13
♖fd1 ♖×d1+ 14 ♖×d1 ♗f5 15
♗×b7 ♖b8 16 ♗c6 ♗×c2 17 ♖c1
♗f5 18 ♘b5 ♗h6

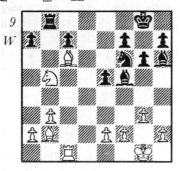

9
W

19 ♖c4 ♗e6 20 ♖a4 ♖d8 21
♗×e5 ♖d1+ 22 ♔g2 ♖c1 23 ♗f3
♘d5 24 ♘d4 ♗g7 25 ♗×g7
♔×g7 26 ♖×a7 ♔f6 27 ♘×e6 fe
28 ♖a5 ♘c3 29 a4 e5 30 ♖c5 1–0

10 Tal–Korchnoi
24th USSR Ch. 1957

1 e4 e6 2 d4 d5 3 ♘c3 ♘c6 4 ♘f3
♗b4 5 e5 b6 6 ♗d3 ♕d7 7 ♗d2
♗b7 8 0–0 ♗f8 9 a3 f5 10 ef gf 11
♕e2 0 0–0 12 ♖fe1 ♖e8 13 ♗f5
♘d8 14 a4 ♘h6 15 ♗h3 a6 16
♘a2 ♔b8 17 ♘b4 ♗×b4 18
♗×b4 ♕g7 19 a5 b5 20 b3 ♖hg8
21 c4 ♗c6 22 g3 ♘f5 23 cb ♗×b5
24 ♕c2 ♘c6 25 ♗c5 ♕d7 26 ♗f1
♗×f1 27 ♖×f1 ♘d6 28 ♗×d6 cd
29 ♖fc1 ♔b7 30 ♕d2 ♖c8

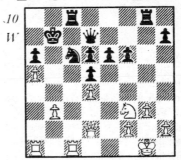

10
W

31 ♖c2 ♘a7 32 ♖ac1 ♖×c2 33
♖×c2 ♘b5 34 ♕f4 ♕e7 35 ♕c1
♕d7 36 ♕f4 ♖g7 37 ♔g2 ♖f7 38
♕h6 ♕e8 39 ♕e3 ♖e7 40 ♖e2
♕g6 41 ♘h4 ♕h5 ½–½

11 Tal–Korchnoi
25th USSR Ch. 1958

1 e4 e6 2 d4 d5 3 ♘c3 ♗b4 4 e5 c5 5
a3 ♗×c3+ 6 bc ♘e7 7 ♕g4 ♘f5 8
♗d3 h5 9 ♕h3 cd 10 ♘f3 ♕c7 11
♖b1 dc 12 g4 ♘e7 13 gh ♘bc6 14

♗f4 ♘g6 15 ♗g3 ♘g×e5 16
♘×e5 ♘×e5 17 ♔f1 ♗d7 18 ♕h4
f6 19 ♗×e5 ♕×e5 20 ♖×b7 ♖b8
21 ♖×b8+ ♕×b8 22 ♕g4 ♔f8 23
♖g1 g5 24 hg ♔g7 25 h4 a5 26
♖g3 ♕b1+ 27 ♔g2 ♕b7 28 h5
d4+ 29 ♗e4 ♗c6 30 ♗×c6
♕×c6+ 31 ♔g1 ♕d5 32 ♕f4 ♕e5

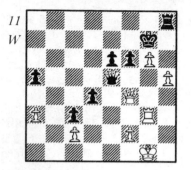

33 h6+ ♖×h6 34 ♕×h6+ ♔×h6
35 g7 ♕×g3+ 0–1

12 Korchnoi–Ivkov
USSR–Yugoslavia 1958

1 d4 ♘f6 2 c4 e6 3 g3 ♗b4+ 4 ♘d2
c5 5 dc 0–0 6 ♗g2 ♘c6 7 ♘f3
♗×c5 8 0–0 b6 9 e4 e5 10 b3 d6 11
♗d2 ♗g4 12 h3 ♗×f3 13 ♗×f3 a5
14 a3 ♘e8 15 ♕d5 ♕c8 16 ♗c3
♘f6 17 ♕d3 ♕b7 18 ♖fe1 ♘h5 19
♕d2 h6 20 b4

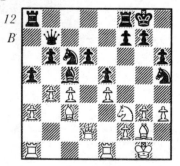

20 ... ab 21 ab ♖×a1 22 ♖×a1
♘×g3 23 bc ♘×e4 24 ♕c2 ♗×c3
25 cd ♕d7 26 ♕×c3 ♕×d6 27
♕d2 ♕f6 28 ♖e1 ♖d8 29 ♕b2
♕f4 30 ♕×b6 ♖d6 31 ♕e3 ♕×c4
32 ♘×e5 ♘×e5 33 ♕×e5 ♖e6 34
♕b8+ ♔h7 35 ♕b1+ g6 36 ♖c1
♕f4 37 ♖c2 ♕f5 38 ♖b2 ♕a5 39
♖b4 ♖e5 40 h4 h5 41 ♗f3 ♖f5 42
♗e4 ♖f6 43 ♕b2 ♖e6 44 ♖b7
♕e5 45 ♖×f7+ ♔g8 46 ♕×e5
♖×e5 47 ♗×g6 1–0

13 Tal–Korchnoi
26th USSR Ch. 1959

1 e4 c5 2 ♘f3 d6 3 d4 cd 4 ♘×d4
♘f6 5 ♘c3 a6 6 ♗g5 ♘bd7 7 ♗c4
♕a5 8 ♕d2 e6 9 0–0 h6 10 ♗h4
♗e7 11 ♖ad1 ♘e5 12 ♗b3 g5 13
♗g3 ♘h5 14 ♗a4+ b5 15 ♗×e5
de 16 ♘c6 ♕c7 17 ♘×e7 ♔×e7 18
♗b3 ♘f6 19 ♕e3 ♗b7 20 a4 b4 21
♘a2 a5 22 c3 ♗a6 23 ♖fe1 bc 24
♖c1 ♖ab8 25 ♖×c3 ♕b6 26
♕×b6 ♖×b6 27 ♖c7+ ♔d6 28
♖a7 ♗b7 29 ♗c4 ♖a8 30 ♖d1+
♔e7 31 ♖×a8 ♗×a8 32 ♗b5
♗×e4 33 b4 ab 34 ♘×b4 ♗b7 35
♘d3 e4 36 ♘e5 ♗d5 37 ♖b1 ♖b8
38 ♖c1 ♖b7 39 ♔f1 ♘e8 40 ♖d1
♘c7 41 ♗e2

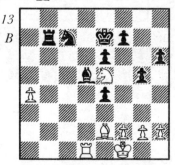

41 ... f6 42 ♘g4 f5 43 ♘e5 ♖b2 44

罝c1 罝a2 45 ♘g6+ ♔d6 46 ♘h8
e5 47 罝d1 ♔e6 48 ♗h5 ♔f6 49
♗f7 ♗×f7 50 ♘×f7 ♔×f7 51
罝d7+ ♔e6 52 罝×c7 f4 53 罝c6+
♔d5 54 罝×h6 f3 55 gf ef 56 ♔e1
罝×a4 57 罝b6 罝a1+ 58 ♔d2 罝f1
59 ♔e3 g4 60 罝b5+ ♔c4 0–1

14 Sakharov–Korchnoi
27th USSR Ch. 1960

1 e4 c5 2 ♘f3 d6 3 d4 cd 4 ♘×d4
♘f6 5 ♘c3 a6 6 ♗g5 c6 7 f4 ♘bd7
8 ♕f3 ♕c7 9 0–0–0 ♗e7 10 g4 b5
11 ♗g2 ♗b7 12 罝he1 ♘b6 13
♗×f6 ♗×f6 14 g5 ♗e7 15 h4 b4 16
♘ce2 g6 17 ♔b1 d5 18 e5 ♘a4 19
h5 ♕b6 20 罝h1 0–0–0 21 hg hg 22
罝h6 ♔b8 23 罝dh1 罝hf8 24 罝h7
a5 25 罝g7 ♗a6 26 罝hh7 ♗c5 27
♘b3 罝d7 28 ♗f1 罝b7 29 ♘ec1
♗×f1 30 ♕×f1 ♗d4 31 ♘d3

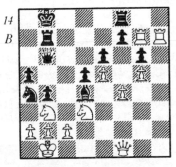

31 ... ♗×b2 32 ♘×b2 ♘c3+ 33
♔a1 a4 34 ♘c1 ♕d4 35 罝h2 a3 36
♘bd3 ♘d1+ 37 ♔b1 ♘c3+ 38
♔a1 ♘e2+ 39 ♔b1 ♘×c1 40
♕×c1 b3 41 cb ♕×d3+ 42 ♕c2
♕d4 43 ♕d2 ♕g1+ 44 ♔c2
罝c7+ 45 ♔d3 ♕b1+ 0–1

15 Smyslov–Korchnoi
27th USSR Ch. 1960

1 d4 ♘f6 2 c4 g6 3 g3 c6 4 ♗g2 d5 5
cd cd 6 ♘f3 ♗g7 7 ♘c3 0–0 8 0–0
♘c6 9 ♘e5 e6 10 ♘×c6 bc 11 ♗f4
♘d7 12 ♘a4 ♗a6 13 罝c1 ♕a5 14
b3 罝fc8 15 ♗d6 ♗b5 16 ♘c3
♕b6 17 ♗c5 ♘×c5 18 dc ♕×c5 19
♘×d5 ♕a3 20 ♘c3 ♗×c3 21
罝×c3 ♕×a2 22 ♗f3 罝d8 23 ♕c1
罝ac8 24 ♕e3 ♕d2 25 ♕c5 ♕d4
26 罝fc1 ♕×c5 27 罝×c5 a6 28
♔g2 ♔f8 29 罝1c3 ♔e7 30 e4 ♔d6
31 e5+ ♔c7 32 罝e3 ♔b6 33 罝cc3
罝d2 34 罝e4 罝cd8 35 罝f4 罝8d7
36 h4 罝2d4 37 ♗c4 c5 38 ♔h3 a5
39 ♔g4 h6 40 f3 ♗c6 41 罝e3
♗×e4 42 fe a4 43 ba c4 44 罝f1
罝d3 45 ♗f3 ♗a5 46 罝×d3 cd 47
♔e3 d2 48 罝d1 ♗×a4 49 罝×d2
罝×d2 50 ♔×d2 ♗b3 51 ♔d3

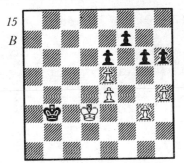

51 ... h5 52 ♔e2 ♔c2 53 ♔e3
♔c3 54 ♔f3 ♔d3 0–1

16 Polugayevsky–Korchnoi
27th USSR Ch. 1960

1 d4 ♘f6 2 c4 g6 3 ♘c3 d5 4 ♘f3
♗g7 5 ♕b3 dc 6 ♕×c4 0–0 7 e4
♘a6 8 ♗e2 c5 9 d5 e6 10 0–0 ed 11
ed ♗f5 12 a3 罝e8 13 罝d1 ♘e4 14
♗e3 ♘d6 15 ♕f4 ♘e4 16 ♘b5
♗×b2 17 罝a2 ♗g7 18 ♗c4 ♘f6
19 ♘d6 ♘h5 20 ♘×b7 ♕c8 21
♕d6

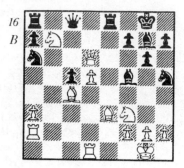

21 ... ♘b8 22 ♗b5 ♖×e3 23 fe
♗f8 24 ♕d8 ♕×b7 25 ♗c4 ♘c6
26 ♕h4 ♘a5 27 ♗f1 ♕b3 28
♖ad2 ♕×e3+ 29 ♔h1 ♗c7 30
♕a4 ♕c3 31 d6 ♗f6 32 d7 ♖d8 33
♖e2 ♔g7 34 ♔g1 ♕b3 35 ♕×b3
♘×b3 36 h3 ♘g3 37 ♖e3 ♘×f1 38
♖×b3 ♗c2 0–1

17 Korchnoi–Krogius
27th USSR Ch. 1960

1 d4 ♘f6 2 c4 e6 3 ♘c3 ♗b4 4 e3
0–0 5 ♘f3 c5 6 ♗e2 d5 7 0–0 ♘c6 8
cd ed 9 dc ♗×c5 10 b3 a6 11 ♘a4
♗a7 12 ♗b2 ♘e4 13 ♖c1 ♗g4 14
♘c3 ♗e6 15 ♗d3 ♘f6 16 ♘e2
♖c8 17 ♘f4 ♖e8 18 ♘g5 d4 19
♕c2 ♘e5 20 ♗×h7+ ♔h8 21
♕b1 ♖×c1 22 ♖×c1 ♘fg4 23
♘f×e6 fe

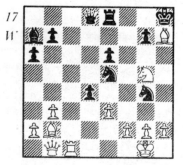

24 ♗g8 g6 25 ♘f7+ ♘×f7 26

♗×f7 ♕h4 27 ♕×g6 ♕×f2+ 28
♔h1 ♕×b2 29 ♕h5+ ♔g7 30
♕×g4+ ♔×f7 31 ♖c7+ ♖e7 32
♕h5+ ♔f6 33 ♕h6+ ♔f5 34 g4+
♔×g4 35 ♕f4+ ♔h5 36 ♖×e7
♕b1+ 37 ♔g2 ♕g6+ 38 ♔h3 1–0

18 Geller–Korchnoi
27th USSR Championship 1960
Alekhine's Defence

In my chess career there have
been many interesting moments,
and many beautiful, fascinating
games. But this game is the one that
is dearest to my heart. Played
towards the end of a very hard
tournament, it is imbued from
beginning to end with fighting
spirit.

1 e4 ♘f6

The game was played in the
penultimate round. Geller was
leading in the tournament, and I
was half a point behind. The choice
of opening was quite in accordance
with my ventursome mood;
although Alekhine's Defence is not
completely sound, it is a fighting
opening. It is no accident that it is
occasionally adopted by Fischer,
Larsen, Hort. . . .

2 e5 ♘d5 3 d4 d6 4 c4 ♘b6 5 f4

The Four Pawns' Attack is an
active rejoinder to Alekhine's
Defence. However, the view of
modern theory (at the end of the
seventies) is that 4 ♘f3 is the most
unpleasant continuation for Black.

5 . . . ♗f5 6 ♘c3 de 7 fe e6 8 ♘f3
♗e7 9 ♗e2 0–0 10 0–0 f6

Black plays the opening not quite
'according to the rules', refraining
for the time being from developing

his knight at c6: the variation 8 . . . ♘c6 9 ♗e3 ♗e7 10 d5 leads to great complications, which at that time were assessed by theory as being clearly favourable for White.

11 ♗f4?!

The usual place for the bishop in this system is at e3. After 11 ef ♗×f6 12 ♗e3 ♘c6 13 ♕d2 ♕d7 14 ♖ad1 White stands slightly better in view of his advantage in space. But the absence of the knight from c6 suggests to Geller the idea of finding a better post for his bishop. But his idea is in fact dubious.

11 . . . ♘c6 12 ef ♗×f6 13 d5 ♘a5 14 ♘e5

Evidently Geller had earlier intended to play differently in this position: for instance, 14 d6 cd 15 ♗×d6, but he did not like the position after 15 . . . ♖f7 16 c5 ♘bc4. Indeed, Black's threats – ♘×b2, ♘e3 and ♘×d6 appear difficult to meet. The tempting 14 ♘d4 also fails, to 14 . . . ♘a×c4 15 ♘×c6 ♗×e6 16 de ♘×b2, when White has no real compensation for the sacrificed pawn. But the position of the knight at e5 also has its drawbacks.

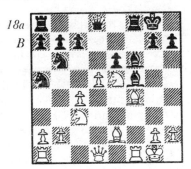

14 . . . ♗×e5?

A mistake typical for me in the early stage of my chess career; in striving to win material as early as possible, I overlook (or under-estimate) an answering counter-blow by my opponent. The correct move 14 . . . ♕e7!, with the threat of 15 . . . ♗×e5 16 ♗×e5 ♘a×c4, would have given Black the advantage. In the event of 14 . . . ♕e7 15 ♕d4, very strong is 15 . . . ♖ad8, with the threat of 16 . . . ♘c6!.

15 ♗×e5 ♘a×c4 16 ♗×c4 ♘×c4 17 ♗×g7!

It is difficult to admit this to the reader, or even to myself, but I overlooked this move! King safety is one of the most important factors in the middle game, and therefore the loss of the pawn at g7 is bound to give White the advantage if the game should continue quietly. Thus after 17 . . . ♔×g7 18 ♕d4+ ♕f6 19 ♕×c4 ♖f7 20 ♖ae1 White has an undisputed advantage. Black is forced to throw caution to the winds.

17 . . . ♘e3! 18 ♕e2

This isn't bad, but the alternative – 18 ♕d4 ♕g5 19 ♖f2 was perhaps safer. In the event of 19 . . . ♖f7 20 ♗e5 ♘c2 21 ♖×c2 ♗×c2 22 de White has a powerful initiative. After 19 . . . ♘c2 20 ♖×c2 ♕×g7 21 ♖d2 ♕×d4 22 ♖×d4 ed Black has quite good chances of equalizing – but that is all. The attempt to win a piece by 19 . . . c5 20 dc ♖ad8 21 ♕e5 ♘g4 is parried by the clever 21 ♗f6!

18 . . . ♘×f1 19 ♗×f8 ♘×h2!

Now Black also succeeds in

weakening the opponent's king position!

20 ♗c5

Not, of course, 20 ♔×h2 ♕h4+ 21 ♔g1 ♖×f8 22 de ♕d4+ 23 ♔h1 ♖f6, and Black wins.

20 ... ♘g4

I think that the objectively strongest continuation here was 20 ... b6 21 de bc 22 e7 ♕d4+ 23 ♔×h2 ♕h4+ 24 ♔g1 ♕d4+ 25 ♕f2 ♔f7, and the resulting ending should finish in a draw. But after all, I was playing 'the game of my life'!

21 de ♕h4 22 e7 ♕h2+

On the immediate 22 ... ♖e8 there could have followed 23 ♕c4+ ♔g7 24 ♕f4, when the white pieces are significantly more actively placed.

23 ♔f1 ♕f4+

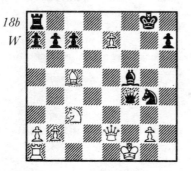

18b
W

24 ♔g1?

Clearly, if Geller had been playing this game normally, with his characteristic energy, he would have played 24 ♔e1 and ... forced Black to take a draw by 24 ... ♕g3+ 25 ♔d2 ♕f4+ 26 ♔e1 etc. The point is that in the event of 26 ... ♖e8, 27 ♘d5 is very strong,

e.g. 27 ... ♕g3+ 28 ♔d2 b6 29 ♖f1, and White, bringing his rook into play, wins.

But this is the specific nature of decisive games – the most cast-iron of nerves cannot stand the tension. And here White displays his indecision, and leaves his king in the danger zone. Soon, all Geller's ingenuity is required in order to save the game.

24 ... ♖e8 25 ♕f3

Now after 25 ♘d5 ♕h2+ 26 ♔f1 b6 27 ♗g1 ♕d6 28 ♕f3 ♗c8, or 28 ♖d1 c6, it is White who is in difficulties.

25 ... ♕h2+ 26 ♔f1 ♕h5

26 ... ♕h1+ 27 ♔e2 ♕×a1 would be a mistake – after 28 ♕d5+ ♔g7 29 ♕×f5 White has a winning attack.

27 ♕d5+ ♔g7 28 ♕d4+

Some commentators considered this check to be a mistake, and instead of it suggested the 'developing' move 28 ♖e1. But after 28 ♖e1 ♗d3+! Black has the better chances: 29 ♕×d3 ♕×c5 30 ♕g3 h5, and the pawn at e7 is bound to fall.

28 ... ♔g6 29 ♘e2 ♕h1+ 30 ♘g1?

Evidently the decisive slip. After 30 ♕g1! White was still all right, e.g. 30 ... ♕h4 (which is what I was intending to play at the board) 31 ♘f4+ ♔f7 32 ♕d4, or 30 ... ♕h6 31 ♕d4, and Black cannot strengthen his position.

30 ... b6 31 ♕d8

31 ♗a3 c5 32 ♕d6+ would have been more tenacious.

31 ... ♘f6 32 ♗a3 ♗e4

Now Black's attack is decisive!

33 ♕d2 c5 34 b4 c4 35 b5
♗d3+! White resigns.

19 Korchnoi–Suetin
27th USSR Ch. 1960

1 e4 e5 2 ♘f3 ♘c6 3 ♗b5 a6 4 ♗a4
♘f6 5 0–0 ♘xe4 6 d4 b5 7 ♗b3 d5
8 de ♗e6 9 ♕e2 ♗e7 10 c3 0–0 11
♘d4 ♕d7 12 f3 ♘c5 13 ♗c2 f6 14
ef ♗xf6 15 ♘xe6 ♕xe6 16
♕xe6+ ♘xe6 17 ♗b3 ♖ad8 18
♖d1 ♘e7 19 ♘d2 ♔f7 20 ♖f1 c5
21 f4 c4 22 ♗d1 ♘c6 23 ♘f3 d4 24
♘g5+ ♗xg5 25 fg+ ♔e7 26 ♖e1
♔d6 27 cd ♘exd4 28 ♗d2 ♖de8
29 ♖c1 ♔d5 30 b3 ♖xe1+ 31
♗xc1 ♘e5 32 bc+ bc 33 ♖b1
♖c8 34 ♗c3 ♘b5 35 ♗a1 c3 36 a4
♘d6 37 ♗b3+ ♔e4 38 ♖e1+
♔f5 39 ♗c2+ ♔e6 40 ♗b3+ ♔f5
41 ♗c2+ ♔e6

42 ♖e3 ♘c4 43 ♖xc3 ♖d8 44 h3
g6 45 ♗b3 ♔f5 46 ♔h2 ♖c8 47
♖c2 ♖c6 48 ♖e2 ♖b6 49 ♗c2+
♔e6 50 ♗d4 ♖d6 51 ♗c3 ♖b6 52
♔g3 ♔d5 53 ♔f4 ♘c6 54 ♖e1
♖b7 55 ♗e4+ ♔c5 56 ♖c1 ♖b3
57 ♗g7 ♘b4 58 ♗f8+ ♔d4 59
♖d1+ ♘d3 60 ♖xd3+ ♖xd3 61
♗g7+ 1–0

20 Fischer–Korchnoi
Buenos Aires 1960

1 e4 c5 2 ♘f3 a6 3 d4 cd 4 c3 dc 5
♘xc3 ♘c6 6 ♗c4 d6 7 0–0 ♘f6 8
♗g5 e6 9 ♕e2 ♗e7 10 ♖fd1 ♕c7
11 ♖ac1 0–0 12 ♗b3 h6 13 ♗f4 e5
14 ♗e3 ♕d8 15 ♘d5 ♘xd5 16
♗xd5 ♗d7 17 ♘d2 ♘b4 18 ♗b3
♗g5 19 ♗xg5 ♕xg5

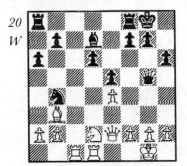

20 ♘f3 ♗g4 21 ♖c7 ♕d8 22
♖xb7 ♖b8 23 ♖xb8 ♕xb8 24 h3
♗xf3 25 ♕xf3 ♘c6 26 ♕d3 ♘d4
27 ♗c4 a5 28 b3 ♕b4 29 f4 ♔h7
½–½

21 Korchnoi–Botvinnik
Leningrad–Moscow 1960

1 d4 ♘f6 2 c4 e6 3 ♘c3 ♗b4 4 e3
b6 5 ♘e2 ♘e4 6 ♕c2 ♗b7 7 a3
♗xc3+ 8 ♘xc3 f5 9 b3 0–0 10
♗b2 d6 11 d5 ♘xc3 12 ♕xc3 e5
13 f4 ♘d7 14 ♗d3 ♕h4+ 15 g3
♕h6 16 0–0 c6 17 dc ♗xc6 18 ♕c2
♖ae8(21)

19 ♗xf5 ♘c5 20 b4 ♗a4 21
♗xh7+ ♕xh7 22 ♕xh7+ ♔xh7
23 bc ef 24 cb ab 25 ef ♖e4 26
♖ae1 ♖fe8 27 ♔f2 ♖xc4 28
♖xe8 ♗xe8 29 ♖c1 ♖xc1 30
♗xc1 g6 31 g4 ♔g7 32 ♔g3 ♗c6
33 ♔h4 ♗g2 34 ♔g5 ♗h3 35

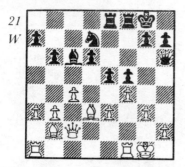

♗b2+ ♔f7 36 a4 ♗g2 37 h4 ♗c6
38 h5 gh 39 ♔×h5 ♗×a4 40 f5
♗d1 41 ♔g5 b5 42 ♗c3 1–0

22 Spassky–Korchnoi
28th USSR Ch. 1961

1 e4 c5 2 ♘f3 a6 3 ♘c3 e6 4 d4 cd 5
♘×d4 ♘c6 6 ♗e3 ♘f6 7 ♗d3
♕c7 8 0–0 ♘×d4 9 ♗×d4 ♗c5 10
♗e2 d6 11 ♗×c5 ♕×c5 12 ♕d3
b5 13 ♖ad1 ♔e7 14 a3 ♗b7 15
♖d2 ♖ac8 16 ♖fd1 ♖hd8 17
♕d4 ♕×d4 18 ♖×d4

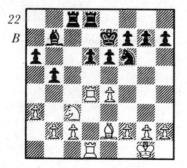

18 . . . e5 19 ♖b4 d5 20 ed ♘×d5
21 ♘×d5 ♗×d5 22 c3 f5 23 ♔f1
♗c6 24 g3 ♖×d1+ 25 ♗×d1 f4 26
♔e1 g5 27 ♗e2 ♖d8 28 a4 a5 29
♖b3 ba 30 ♖b6 ♗d7 31 f3 fg 32 hg
h5 33 ♖g6 ♖b8 34 ♖×g5 ♔f6 35
f4 ♖×b2 36 ♖×e5 a3 37 ♗c4 a2 38

♗×a2 ♖×a2 39 ♖×h5 a4 40 ♖a5
♗e6 0–1

23 Korchnoi–Polugayevsky
28th USSR Ch. 1961

1 d4 ♘f6 2 c4 e6 3 ♘c3 ♗b4 4 e3
0–0 5 ♗d3 d5 6 ♘f3 c5 7 0–0 dc 8
♗×c4 ♘bd7 9 ♕d3 ♕e7 10 a3
♗a5 11 dc ♘×c5 12 ♕c2 ♗×c3 13
♕×c3 ♗d7 14 b4 ♘a4 15 ♕e5
♘b6 16 ♗a2 ♗c6 17 ♗b2 ♗×f3
18 gf ♖ac8 19 ♖fc1 ♖fd8 20 f4 h6
21 f5 ♘bd7 22 ♕b5 ♖×c1+ 23
♖×c1 ♘f8 24 fe fe 25 ♗d4 ♘d5

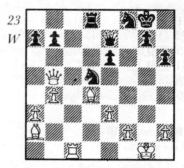

26 ♕f1 ♘g6 27 ♕h3 ♘gf4 28 ♕g4
h5 29 ♕f3 ♘d3 30 ♖f1 ♖f8 31
♕×h5 ♖f5 32 ♕e2 ♘e5 33 f4 ♘c6
34 ♗b2 ♕f7 35 ♗b1 ♖h5 36 ♖f2
♘ce7 37 ♖g2 ♘f5 38 ♗×f5 ♕×f5
39 e4 ♘×f4 40 ef ♘×e2+ 41 ♖×e2
1–0

24 Korchnoi–Bilek
European Team Ch. Oberhausen
1961

1 c4 ♘f6 2 ♘c3 e6 3 ♘f3 ♗b4 4 a3
♗×c3 5 bc d6 6 g3 b6 7 ♗g2 ♗b7 8
0–0 ♘bd7 9 d3 0–0 10 e4 ♘e8 11
h4 ♘c5 12 ♘d4 ♕d7 13 ♖e1 ♔h8
14 ♖a2 ♘f6 15 f4 ♕a4 16 ♕f3

♘fd7 17 ♕e2 a6 18 ♖b2 ♕×a3 19 ♕d2 e5 20 ♖a2

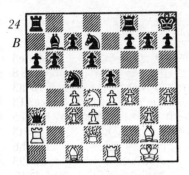

20 ... ♕×a2 21 ♕×a2 ♘×d3 22 ♖d1 ♘3c5 23 ♕c2 ♖ae8 24 ♘f5 g6 25 ♘h6 ♔g7 26 f5 ♘f6 27 ♖e1 ♘h5 28 ♗f3 ♘×g3 29 ♔f2 gf 30 ef e4 31 ♗g4 ♘d3+ 32 ♔×g3 ♘×e1 33 ♕d2 e3 34 ♕×e1 ♔×h6 35 f6 ♔g6 36 ♕f1 ♖e5 37 h5+ 1–0

25 Korchnoi–Bilek
Budapest 1961

1 e4 c5 2 ♘f3 g6 3 d4 ♗g7 4 c4 d6 5 ♘c3 ♘c6 6 ♗e3 ♕a5 7 d5 ♘e5 8 ♘×e5 ♗×e5 9 ♗d2 a6 10 ♗d3 ♕c7 11 f4 ♗d4 12 ♕c2 ♘h6 13 ♘e2 ♗g7 14 h3 f5 15 ef ♘×f5 16 g4 ♘d4 17 ♘×d4 cd 18 f5 gf 19 ♗×f5 ♗×f5 20 ♕×f5 ♖f8 21 ♕×h7

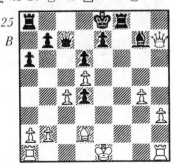

21 ... ♕×c4 22 ♕g6+ ♖f7 23 ♕e6 ♕d3 24 ♖c1 ♕g3+ 25 ♔d1 ♕f3+ 26 ♔c2 ♖f6 27 ♖hf1 ♖×e6 28 ♖×f3 ♖e5 29 g5 ♖×d5 30 h4 ♔d7 31 h5 d3+ 32 ♔b1 ♖g8 33 h6 ♗h8 34 ♖h1 ♔e8 35 ♖hf1 ♗e5 36 h7 ♖h8 37 g6 ♖d4 38 ♗c3 ♖g4 39 ♗×e5 de 40 ♖f8+ ♖×f8 41 ♖×f8+ ♔d7 42 ♖f1 1–0

26 Korchnoi–Simagin
Budapest 1961

1 c4 e6 2 ♘c3 ♘f6 3 ♘f3 d5 4 d4 ♗e7 5 ♗g5 0–0 6 e3 ♘bd7 7 ♗d3 c6 8 0–0 b6 9 cd ed 10 ♖b1 ♗b7 11 b4 ♖e8 12 ♕b3 b5 13 a4 a5

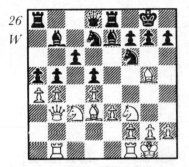

14 ♗×f6 ♘×f6 15 ba b4 16 ♘a2 ♖b8 17 a6 ♗a8 18 ♕c2 ♕b6 19 ♘c1 ♘e4 20 ♘e5 ♖bc8 21 ♗×e4 de 22 ♕c4 ♕d8 23 ♕×f7+ ♔h8 24 ♘b3 ♗d6 25 ♘c4 ♖c7 1–0

27 Fischer–Korchnoi
Stockholm Interzonal 1962

1 e4 e5 2 ♘f3 ♘c6 3 ♗b5 a6 4 ♗a4 ♘f6 5 0–0 ♗e7 6 ♖e1 b5 7 ♗b3 0–0 8 c3 d6 9 d4 ♗g4 10 ♗e3 ed 11 cd ♘a5 12 ♗c2 ♘c4 13 ♗c1 c5 14 b3 ♘a5 15 d5 ♘d7 16 ♘bd2 ♗f6 17 ♖b1 c4 18 h3 ♗×f3 19 ♘×f3 cb

20 ab ♕c7 21 ♗e3 ♗c3 22 ♖e2 b4 23 ♘d4

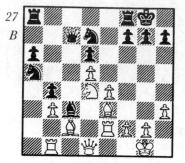

27
B

23 ... ♖fe8 24 ♘f5 ♘b7 25 ♗d4 g6 26 ♘h6+ ♔f8 27 ♖c1 ♖ac8 28 ♗d3 ♕a5 29 ♖ec2 ♘e5 30 ♗f1 ♘c5 31 ♗×c3 bc 32 ♖×c3 ♔g7 33 ♘g4 ♘×g4 34 ♕×g4 ♖b8 35 ♖f3 ♘×e4 36 ♕f4 f5 37 ♖e3 ♖e5 38 ♖c6 ♖be8 39 ♖×d6 ♕a1 40 ♖×a6 ♕d4 41 ♖d3 ♕b2 42 d6 g5 43 ♕e3 f4 44 ♕a7+ 1–0

28 Korchnoi–Stein
30th USSR Ch. 1962

1 d4 ♘f6 2 c4 g6 3 ♘c3 d5 4 ♘f3 ♗g7 5 ♗f4 0–0 6 ♖c1 c5 7 dc dc 8 ♕×d8 ♖×d8 9 e3 Na6 10 c6 bc 11 ♗×c4 ♘d5 12 ♗e5 ♘b6 13 ♗e2 f6 14 ♗g3 e5 15 0–0 ♘c5 16 b4

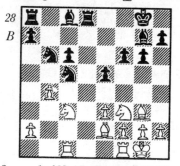

28
B

16 ... ♘d3? 17 ♖cd1 ♗f5 18 e4 ♘×b4 19 ef gf 20 ♘d2 f4 21 ♗h4

♘6d5 22 ♘db1 ♔f7 23 ♖c1 ♗f8 24 ♘e4 ♖dc8 25 ♗h5+ ♔g7 26 ♗g4 ♖c7 27 ♗e6 ♖e8 28 ♗×d5 ♘×d5 29 ♖fd1 ♖ec8 30 ♘bc3 ♗e7 31 ♔f1 ♘×c3 32 ♖×c3 ♖b8 33 ♘c5 ♖cc8 34 ♖d7 ♔f7 35 ♖×a7 ♖d8 36 ♘b3 ♖d6 37 f3 ♖bd8 38 ♗f2 ♖d1+ 39 ♔e2 ♔e8 40 ♖×c6 1–0

29 Spassky–Korchnoi
30th USSR Ch. 1962

1 d4 ♘f6 2 c4 e6 3 ♘f3 d5 4 ♘c3 c5 5 cd ♘×d5 6 e3 ♘c6 7 ♗c4 cd 8 ed ♗e7 9 0–0 0–0 10 ♖e1 a6 11 ♗d3 ♘f6 12 ♗g5 b5 13 ♖c1 ♗b7 14 ♗b1 ♖c8 15 a3 ♘a5 16 ♕d3 g6 17 ♗h6 ♖e8 18 ♘e5 ♘c4 19 ♘×c4 bc 20 ♕d2 ♕b6 21 ♗f4 ♖ed8 22 ♗e5 ♗g4 23 ♕e2 ♘×e5 24 de ♖d4 25 ♗e4 ♖cd8 26 ♗×b7 ♕×b7 27 ♘e4 ♕b5 28 ♘c3 ♕b8 29 ♖c2 ♖d3 30 g3 ♖8d4 31 ♘d1 ♕b3 32 ♘e3 ♗g5 33 ♘f1 (28)

33 ... a5 34 f4 ♗e7 35 ♖ec1 ♗c5 36 ♔h1 ♕b7+ 37 ♕g2 ♕d5 38 a4 ♖f3 39 ♘d2 ♖f2 40 ♕×d5 ed 41 ♘f1 ♖d3 42 ♖c3 ♖×c3 43 bc d4 44 cd ♗×d4 0–1

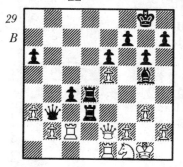

29
B

30 Korchnoi–Tal
30th USSR Ch. 1962

1 d4 ♘f6 2 c4 c5 3 d5 e6 4 ♘c3 ed 5

cd d6 6 ♘f3 g6 7 g3 ♗g7 8 ♗g2
0–0 9 0–0 ♘a6 10 h3 ♘c7 11 e4
♘d7 12 ♖e1 ♘e8 13 ♗g5 ♗f6 14
♗e3 ♖b8 15 a4 a6 16 ♗f1 ♕e7 17
♘d2 ♘c7 18 f4 b5 19 e5 de 20
♘de4 ♕d8 21 ♘×f6+ ♘×f6 22 d6
♘e6 23 fe b4 24 ♘d5 ♘×d5 25
♕×d5 ♗b7 26 ♕d2 ♕d7 27 ♔h2
b3 28 ♖ac1 ♕×a4 29 ♗c4 ♗c8 30
♖f1 ♖b4 31 ♗×e6 ♗×e6 32 ♗h6
♖e8 33 ♕g5 ♖e4 34 ♖f2 f5 35 ♕f6
♕d7 36 ♖×c5 ♖c4 37 ♖×c4
♗×c4 38 ♖d2 ♗e6 39 ♖d1 ♕a7
40 ♖d2 ♕d7 41 ♖d1 ♕a7 42 ♖d4
♕d7 43 g4 a5 44 ♔g3 ♖b8 45
♔h4 ♕f7 46 ♔g5 fg 47 hg ♗d7 48
♖c4 a4 49 ♖c7 a3

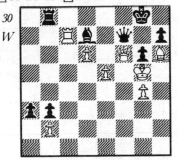

30
W

50 ♖×d7 ♕×d7 51 e6 ♕a7 52
♕e5 ab 53 e7 ♔f7 54 d7 1–0

31 Korchnoi–Robatsch
Havana 1963

1 d4 ♘f6 2 c4 e6 3 ♘f3 d5 4 ♗g5 h6
5 ♗×f6 ♕×f6 6 ♘c3 c6 7 e3 ♘d7 8
♗d3 ♗b4 9 0–0 ♕c7 10 ♖c1 0–0
11 a3 ♗d6 12 c5 ♗c7 13 e4 de 14
♗×e4 e5 15 d5 ♘×c5 16 dc ♖d8
17 ♘d5 ♕d6 18 ♘×c7 ♕×c7 (*31*)
   19 ♖×c5 ♖×d1 20 cb ♖×f1+ 21
♔×f1 ♕×b7 22 ♗×b7 ♗×b7 23
♘×e5 ♖d8 24 b4 ♖d1+ 25 ♔e2
♖a1 26 ♖a5 a6 27 g3 ♗g2 28 ♘d3
♗f1+ 29 ♔d2 ♔h7 30 ♖×a6

♖b1 31 ♔c2 ♖a1 32 b5 ♗e2 33 b6
1–0

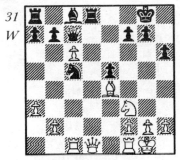

31
W

32 Trifunovic–Korchnoi
Havana 1963

1 d4 ♘f6 2 ♘f3 e6 3 ♗g5 h6 4 ♗h4
g5 5 ♗g3 d6 6 ♘bd2 ♘h5 7 e3
♗g7 8 c3 f5 9 ♗c4 ♕e7 10 ♘g1
♘f6 11 f4 ♘c6 12 ♘f3 ♗d7 13
♕e2 0–0–0 14 0–0–0 ♘h5 15
♖he1 ♖he8 16 ♗b5 a6 17 ♗d3
♔b8 18 ♔b1 ♗f6 19 fg hg 20 ♗f2
g4 21 ♘g1 e5 22 d5 ♘a7 23 e4 ♘f4
24 ♕e3 ♘c8 25 ♗f1 ♗g5 26 ♕g3
♖h8 27 h3

32
B

27 ... ♘h5 28 ♕d3 g3 29 ♗×g3
♘×g3 30 ♕×g3 ♗h4 31 ♕e3
♗×e1 32 ♖×e1 ♕g7 33 ♔c1 ♘e7
34 c4 ♖hg8 35 ♘gf3 fe 36 ♘×e4
♘f5 37 ♕d2 ♘g3 38 ♗d3 ♘×e4
39 ♗×e4 ♕×g2 40 ♕×g2 ♖×g2
41 ♘×e5 ♖h2 42 ♘×d7+ ♖×d7

43 ♗d3 ♖g7 44 ♖e8+ ♔a7 45
♗e2 ♖×h3 46 ♔d2 a5 47 ♗d3
♖g2+ 48 ♗e2 ♔b6 49 ♖e7 ♔c5
50 ♖×c7+ ♔d4 51 ♖e7 ♖d3+ 52
♔c1 ♖e3 53 ♖×e3 ♔×e3 54 ♗d1
b6 55 c5 bc 56 ♗a4 ♔d3 57 ♗b5+
c4 58 b3 ♔c3 0–1

33 Korchnoi–Suetin
31st USSR Ch. 1963

1 ♘f3 c5 2 g3 ♘c6 3 d4 cd 4 ♘×d4
g6 5 ♗g2 ♗g7 6 ♘b3 ♘f6 7 e4 0–0
8 ♘c3 d6 9 h3 ♗e6 10 ♘d5 a5 11
a4 ♘b4 12 c3 ♘b×d5 13 ed ♗d7
14 ♘d4 ♕c8 15 ♕b3 ♘e8 16 ♗e3
♘c7 17 h4 ♘a6 18 0–0 ♘c5 19
♕c2 ♕e8 20 b3 ♖c8 21 ♕d1 ♕d8
22 ♖b1 ♕c7 23 ♖e1 ♖fe8 24 ♖c1
h5 25 ♗f1 ♘e4 26 ♗b5 ♘f6 27 c4
♘g4 28 ♗×d7 ♕×d7 29 ♖c2 ♘e5
30 ♗f4 ♕g4 31 f3 ♕d7 32 ♔g2
♕d8 33 ♖ce2 ♕d7 34 ♖e4 ♗f6 35
♘b5 ♖a8 36 ♕e2 ♗g7 37 ♗c1
♔f8 38 ♗a3 b6

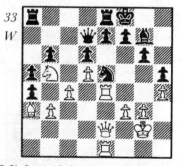

33
W

39 f4 ♘g4 40 ♘×d6 f5 41 ♘×e8 fe
42 ♘×g7 ♔×g7 43 ♕×e4 ♖e8 44
♕×e7+ 1–0

34 Korchnoi–Polugayevsky
31st USSR Ch. 1963

1 c4 e5 2 ♘c3 ♘c6 3 g3 g6 4 ♗g2
♗g7 5 e3 d6 6 ♘ge2 ♗d7 7 d4

♕c8 8 d5 ♘ce7 9 e4 h5 10 ♘g1
♘h6 11 ♕e2 f5 12 f4 ♘f7 13 ♘f3
0–0 14 0–0 fe 15 ♘×e4 ♘f5 16
♗d2 ♕d8 17 ♖ae1 c6 18 fe ♘×e5
19 ♘×e5 ♗×e5 20 dc bc 21 ♗c3
♗×c3 22 bc ♕e7 23 ♕d2 ♖ae8

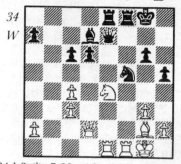

34
W

24 h3 ♔g7 25 g4 hg 26 hg ♘h4 27
g5 ♖×f1+ 28 ♖×f1 ♖×c4 29
♗×e4 ♘f5 30 ♗×f5 ♗×f5 31 ♖e1
♕d7 32 ♕d4 ♗c2 33 ♖e2 ♕f5 34
♕d2 ♗e4 35 ♕e3 ♕g4+ 36 ♔f2
♕f5+ 37 ♔e1 d5 38 ♖f2 ♕g4 39
♕f4 ♕g1+ 40 ♖f1 ♕c5 41 ♕f7+
♔h8 42 ♕e8+ 1–0

35 Korchnoi–Tal
32nd USSR Ch. 1964–65

1 c4 ♘f6 2 ♘c3 e6 3 ♘f3 d5 4 d4 c5
5 cd ♘×d5 6 e3 ♗e7 7 ♗d3 ♘c6 8
0–0 0–0 9 a3 b6 10 ♕c2 g6 11 dc bc
12 ♖d1 ♘×c3 13 ♕×c3 ♖b8 14
♗c2 ♕b6 15 ♖b1 ♗a6 16 b3 f5 17
♗b2 ♗f6 18 ♕c1 ♗×b2 19 ♖×b2
♕a5 20 ♕×a5 ♘×a5 21 ♖bb1
♖fd8 22 ♘e5 ♖×d1+ 23 ♗×d1
♖d8 24 b4 cb 25 ab ♘c4 26 ♘c6
♖d7 27 ♖a1 ♗b7 28 ♘×a7 ♖d2
29 ♗b3 ♗d5 30 ♗×c4 ♗×c4 31
♘c6 ♖b2 32 h4 ♗b5 33 ♘d4
♖×b4 34 ♘×e6 ♖×h4 35 ♖a8+
♔f7 36 ♘g5+ ♔g7 37 f4 ♗c6 38
♖a6 ♗d5 39 ♖d6 ♗g8 40 ♖d8
♖h5 41 ♖d7+ ♔f6

35
W

42 e4 fe 43 ♘×e4+ ♔f5 44 ♘g3+
♔×f4 45 ♘×h5+ gh 46 ♔h2 ♗e6
47 ♖×h7 ♔g4 48 ♖e7 ♗f5 49
♖g7+ ♔f4 50 g3+ ♔f3 51 ♖g5
♗g4 52 ♖e5 ♔f2 53 ♖e8 ♗e2 54
♖f8+ ♗f3 55 ♖f7 ♔e3 56 ♔g1
♗e1 57 ♖ff8 ♗d3 58 ♖a8 ♗f5 59
♖a5 ♗g4 60 ♔g2 ♗f3+ 61 ♔f1
♗e2+ 62 ♔e1 ♗g4 63 ♖a3+
♔e4 64 ♔f2 ♗d1 65 ♖a5 ♗g4 66
♖a8 ♔f5 67 ♖d8 ♔e4 68 ♖f8
♗h3 69 ♔e2 ♗g4+ 70 ♔d2 ♗f5
71 ♖f7 ♗g4 72 ♖f4+ ♔e5 73
♔e3 ♗e6 74 ♖f8 ♗h3 75 ♖a8
♔f5 76 ♖a5+ ♔g6 77 ♔f4 h4 78
♖a6+ ♔g7 79 gh ♗f1 80 ♖b6
♗e2 81 ♔g5 ♗d1 82 ♖b7+ ♔g8
83 ♔h6 ♗f3 84 ♖b3 ♗e4 85
♖g3+ ♔f7 86 ♔g5 ♗c2 87 ♔f4
♗g6 88 ♖g5 ♔f6 89 h5 ♗e4 90 h6
♗g6 91 ♖g3 ♗b1 92 ♖g7 ♗g6 93
♖a7 1–0

36 Vasyukov–Korchnoi
32nd USSR Ch. 1964–65

1 e4 e6 2 d4 d5 3 ♘c3 ♗b4 4 e5 c5 5
a3 ♗×c3+ 6 bc ♘e7 7 a4 ♘bc6 8
♘f3 ♗d7 9 ♗e2 f6 10 ef gf 11 dc
♕a5 12 ♕d2 ♕×c5 13 ♗a3 ♕a5
14 0–0 0–0 15 ♖fd1 ♖f7 16 c4
♕×d2 17 ♖×d2 ♖c8 18 a5 ♘g6
19 a6 b6 20 ♖ad1 ♘f4 21 ♗f1

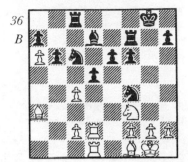

36
B

21 ... e5 22 cd ♘a5 23 g3 ♘h3+
24 ♔g2 ♘c4 25 ♗b4 e4 26 ♘d4
♘×f2 27 ♖e1 ♘×d2 28 ♗×d2
♘g4 29 ♖×e4 ♘e5 30 ♗b4 ♖g7
31 h3 ♗e8 32 c4 ♗g6 33 ♖e1 ♗d3
34 ♘e6 ♖d7 35 ♗c3 ♗×c4 36
♗×e5 ♗×d5+ 37 ♔g1 fe 38
♖×e5 ♗×e6 39 ♖×e6 ♖c1 40
♔g2 ♖d2+ 41 ♗e2 ♔f7 42 ♖e4
♖c6 43 ♔f1 0–1

37 Korchnoi–Lutikov
32nd USSR Ch. 1964–65

1 g3 d5 2 ♘f3 ♘f6 3 ♗g2 c6 4 0–0
♗g4 5 b3 ♘bd7 6 ♗b2 e6 7 c4
♗d6 8 d4 0–0 9 ♘c3 ♕e7 10 ♕c1
♖ac8 11 ♖e1 c5 12 cd ♗×f3 13 dc
♘×c5 14 ♗×f3 ♘ce4 15 ♗×e4
♘×e4 16 ♕e3 ♘×c3 17 ♗×c3 ed

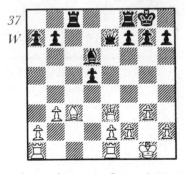

37
W

18 ♕d4 ♕g5 19 ♗d2 ♕f6 20

♕×d5 ♗e5 21 ♖ad1 ♖fd8 22
♕e4 ♖d4 23 ♕b1 h5 24 ♗e3 ♖g4
25 ♕d3 a6 26 ♕d7 ♖c3 27 ♕d8+
♔h7 28 ♕×f6 ♗×f6 29 ♖c1 ♔g6
30 ♗f4 1–0

38 Korchnoi–Sakharov
32nd USSR Ch. 1964–65

1 g3 d5 2 ♘f3 ♘f6 3 ♗g2 c6 4 0–0
♗g4 5 b3 ♘bd7 6 ♗b2 e6 7 d3
♗c5 8 ♘bd2 0–0 9 h3 ♗×f3 10
♘×f3 a5 11 a3 ♕c7 12 c4 ♖fd8 13
♖c1 ♕b6 14 ♕c2 ♗e7 15 ♖b1 h6
16 ♖fc1 ♘h7 17 e3 ♗f6 18 d4 ♗e7
19 c5 ♕c7 20 b4 ab 21 ab b5 22 cb
♕×b6 23 ♗c3 ♖dc8 24 ♘e1 ♘hf6
25 ♘d3 ♘e8 26 ♗f1 ♘d6 27 ♘c5
♕c7 28 ♗e1 ♘b6 29 ♘b3 ♘dc4
30 ♕d1 e5 31 ♘a5 ed 32 ♘×c4 dc
33 ♕×d4 c5 34 bc ♗×c5 35 ♕g4
♗f8 36 ♗c3 ♘a4 37 ♗d4 c3 38
♗g2 ♖ab8 39 ♖a1 ♖b4 40 ♗e4
♖d8

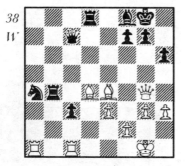

41 ♕f5 g6 42 ♕f6 ♖b×d4 43 ed
♗g7 44 ♕f3 ♖×d4 45 ♖ab1 ♔e7
46 ♖b8+ ♔h7 47 ♖b7 ♖×e4 48
♖×c7 ♖×c7 49 ♕c6 ♘b2 50
♖×c3 ♗×c3 51 ♕×c3 ♘d1 52
♕d2 ♘×f2 53 ♕×f2 h5 54 ♕f6
♖b7 55 ♕c3 ♖b1+ 56 ♔f2 ♔g8
57 ♔e3 ♖b5 58 ♔e4 ♖f5 59 ♕d3

♔h7 60 g4 hg 61 hg ♖g5 62 ♕d7
♔g7 63 ♔f4 ♖a5 64 ♕d4+ ♔h7
65 ♕c4 ♔g8 66 ♕c8+ ♔h7 67
♕f8 ♖a4+ 68 ♔g5 ♖a5+ 69 ♔f6
♖a6+ 70 ♔×f7 ♖a7+ 71 ♔f6
♖a6+ 72 ♔g5 ♖a5+ 73 ♔h4
♖a7 74 ♕c5 ♖b7 75 ♔g5 1–0

39 Petrosian–Korchnoi
Moscow–Leningrad 1965

1 e4 e5 2 ♘f3 ♘c6 3 ♗b5 a6 4 ♗a4
♘f6 5 0–0 ♘×e4 6 d4 b5 7 ♗b3 d5
8 de ♗e6 9 c3 ♗e7 10 ♗f4 ♘c5 11
♗c2 ♗g4 12 h3 ♗h5 13 ♕e2 ♘e6
14 ♗h2 ♗c5 15 ♘bd2 ♘e7 16
♖ad1 ♕c8 17 ♘b3 ♗b6 18 ♔h1
c5 19 g4 ♗g6 20 ♘h4 ♗×c2 21
♕×c2 ♕c6 22 f4

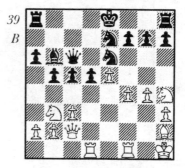

39
B

22 ... d4+ 23 ♕g2 ♕×g2+ 24
♘×g2 dc 25 f5 ♘c7 26 ♗g1 ♘ed5
27 ♘×c5 cb 28 ♖d2 0–0–0 29 ♘e4
♗×g1 30 ♔×g1 ♘b6 31 ♘d6+
♖×d6 32 ed ♘c4 33 d7+ ♔d8 34
♖d3 ♘a8 35 ♘f4 ♖ab6 36 ♖fd1
b4 37 ♘d5 ♘×d5 38 ♖×d5 ♘e3
39 ♖5d3 ♘×d1 40 ♖×d1 ♔c7 41
♖b1 ♔×d7 42 ♖×b2 a5 43 a3 ba
44 ♖a2 ♔c6 45 ♖×a3 ♖a8 46
♔f2 a4 47 ♔e2 ♔b5 48 ♔d2 ♔b4
49 ♖a1 a3 0–1

40 Korchnoi-Petrosian
Moscow–Leningrad 1965

1 d4 ♘f6 2 c4 e6 3 ♘c3 ♗b4 4 e3
0–0 5 ♘f3 c5 6 ♗e2 ♗×c3+ 7 bc
b6 8 ♘d2 ♗b7 9 0–0 d6 10 f3 ♘c6
11 ♘b3 ♘e7 12 e4 ♘g6 13 g3 ♖c8
14 ♖f2 ♗a6 15 d5 ♖e8 16 ♘d2
♕d7 17 a4 ♖e7 18 a5 b5 19 cb
♗×b5 20 c4 ♗a6 21 ♗b2 ♕e8 22
♗f1 ♖b8 23 ♗c3 e5 24 ♗d3 ♗c8
25 ♘f1 ♖eb7 26 ♗c2 a6 27 ♘e3
♘f8 28 ♕f1 h6 29 ♖e1 ♘8h7 30 f4
♘g4 31 ♘×g4 ♗×g4 32 h3 ♗d7
33 ♕g2 f6 34 ♖ef1 ♕d8 35 ♖a1
♕e7 36 ♔f1 ♕e8 37 ♔e2 ♕c8 38
f5

40
B

38 ... ♖b4 39 ♗×b4 cb 40 ♗b3
♕c5 41 ♔f1 ♘g5 42 ♖e2 ♕d4 43
♖b1 ♕d3 44 ♖bb2 ♗c8 45 h4
♘f3 46 ♔f2 ♕d4 47 ♖e3 ♕c3 48
♖×c3 bc 49 ♖b1 ♖×b3 50 ♖×b3
♘×b3 51 ♔e3 ♘d4 52 ♕a2 c2 53
♔d2 ♗h5 54 c5 dc 55 d6+ ♗f7 56
♕a4 1–0

41 Korchnoi-Udovcic
Leningrad 1967

1 d4 e6 2 e4 d5 3 ♘d2 ♘f6 4 e5
♘fd7 5 c3 c5 6 ♘gf3 ♘c6 7 ♗d3
♕b6 8 0–0 cd 9 cd ♘×d4 10 ♘×d4
♕×d4 11 ♘f3 ♕b6 12 ♕a4 ♕b4

13 ♕c2 h6 14 ♗d2 ♕b6 15 ♖ac1
♗e7 16 ♕a4 ♕d8 17 ♖c2 ♔f8 18
♖fc1 ♘b6 19 ♕g4 ♗d7 20 ♗a5
♖c8 21 ♖×c8 ♗×c8 22 ♗b4 g6 23
♕h4 g5 24 ♘×g5 ♔e8 25 ♗b5+
♗d7

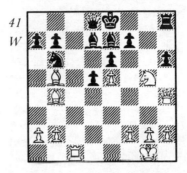

41
W

26 ♘×e6 fe 27 ♕h5+ ♔f8 28 ♖c3
♖h7 29 ♕g6 ♖g7 30 ♕×h6
♗×b5 31 ♖g3 1–0

42 Barczay-Korchnoi
Sousse Interzonal 1967

1 d4 ♘f6 2 c4 e6 3 ♘c3 ♗b4 4 e3
0–0 5 ♗d3 d5 6 ♘f3 c5 7 0–0 ♘c6 8
a3 ♗×c3 9 bc dc 10 ♗×c4 ♕c7 11
♗d3 e5 12 ♘×e5 ♘×e5 13 de
♕×e5 14 ♕c2 ♖d8 15 ♖e1 ♕d5
16 ♗f1 ♗f5 17 ♕b2

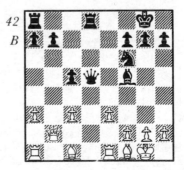

42
B

17 ... ♗d3 18 f3 ♗×f1 19 e4 ♕c4
20 ♖×f1 b6 21 ♗g5 ♖d3 22 ♖ac1
♖ad8 23 e5 h6 24 ef hg 25 ♕e2 gf
26 ♖fe1 ♔g7 27 h3 ♕f4 0–1

43 Miagmasuren–Korchnoi
Sousse Interzonal 1967

1 e4 c5 2 ♘f3 ♘c6 3 ♗b5 g6 4 0–0
♗g7 5 c3 ♘f6 6 e5 ♘d5 7 d4 cd 8
cd 0–0 9 ♘c3 ♘c7 10 ♗a4 d6 11
♗f4 ♗g4 12 ♗×c6 bc 13 h3 ♘e6
14 hg ♘×f4 15 g3 ♘e6 16 ♘e4

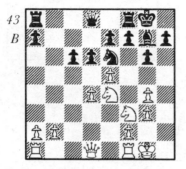

43
B

16 ... ♕a5 17 ed ed 18 g5 ♔h8 19
b3 ♕d5 20 ♖e1 f6 21 gf ♗×f6 22
♖c1 ♗g7 23 ♖e3 ♗h6 24 ♕e2
♗×e3 25 ♕×e3 ♖ad8 0–1

44 Korchnoi–Tal
Wijk aan Zee 1968

1 d4 ♘f6 2 c4 e6 3 ♘c3 ♗b4 4 ♘f3
c5 5 e3 0–0 6 ♗e2 d5 7 a3 cd 8 ab dc
9 bc ♕c7 10 ♕b3 ♗d7 11 ♗b2
♖c8 12 cd ed 13 0–0 ♗e6 14 ♘d4
♘bd7 15 ♖a5 a6 16 ♖fa1 ♖ab8
17 ♕d1 ♘e5 18 ♖c5 ♕b6 19
♘×e6 fe(44)

20 c4 ♘×c4 21 ♗×f6 gf 22
♗×c4 dc 23 ♕g4+ ♔h8 24 ♕d4
♕d8 25 ♕×c4 ♗×c5 26 bc ♕d7
27 ♕f4 ♖f8 28 h4 ♕d5 29 ♖b1 e5

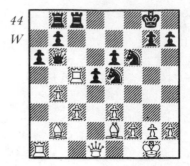

44
W

30 ♕f5 a5 31 ♖b6 a4 32 ♖d6 ♕f7
33 ♖d7 ♕g6 34 ♕e6 ♕b1+ 35
♔h2 ♕e4 36 g3 ♕c2 37 ♔g2
♕e4+ 38 ♔f1 ♕b1+ 39 ♔e2
♕c2+ 40 ♔f3 ♕×c5 41 ♖×b7
♕c8 42 ♖d7 ♕e8 43 ♕×e8 ♖×e8
44 ♖a7 ♖b8 45 h5 ♔g8 46 ♖×a4
♖b7 47 ♔g4 ♔g7 48 ♖a2 ♔h6 49
♔f5 ♖b6 50 e4 ♖c6 51 f4 ef 52 gf
♖c5+ 53 ♔×f6 ♔×h5 54 e5 ♔g4
55 f5 h5 56 ♖a4+ ♔g3 57 e6 h4 58
e7 ♖c8 59 ♔f7 1–0

45 Matanovic–Korchnoi
Wijk aan Zee 1968

1 e4 e6 2 d4 d5 3 ♘d2 c5 4 ed ed 5
♘gf3 a6 6 dc ♗×c5 7 ♘b3 ♗a7 8
♗d3 ♕e7+ 9 ♕e2 ♘c6 10 0–0
♗g4 11 h3 ♗h5 12 ♗f4 ♕×e2 13
♗×e2 ♘f6 14 c3 0–0 15 ♖fe1
♖fe8 16 g4 ♗g6 17 ♗f1 ♖e4 18
♖×e4 ♗×e4 19 ♗g2 h5 20 g5
♘d7 21 ♖d1 ♘f8 22 ♗e3 ♗×e3
23 fe ♘e6 24 h4 ♖e8 25 ♔f2 ♘e7
26 ♗h3 ♗c2(45)

27 ♖a1 ♘g6 28 ♗×e6 fe 29
♔g3 e5 30 ♘bd2 ♘e7 31 ♖e1
♘f5+ 32 ♔h3 ♘d6 33 ♔g2 ♔f7
34 ♘f1 ♔e6 35 ♘g3 g6 36 ♘d2
♖f8 37 ♖e2 b5 38 ♖f2 ♗f5 39 ♔f1
♖c8 40 ♔e1 a5 41 a3 b4 42 ab ab

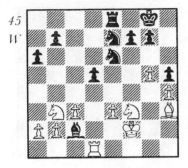

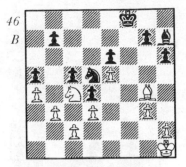

43 ♘e2 ♖a8 44 ♘b3 ♘e4 45 ♖h2
♖b8 46 cb ♖×b4 47 ♘bc1 ♘d6
48 b3 ♘e4 49 ♘g1 ♘c5 50 ♔d1
♘×b3 51 ♖b2 ♖g4 52 ♘ce2 ♘a5
53 ♖b6+ ♔e7 54 ♘f3 ♘c4 55
♖b7+ ♔e6 56 ♔e1 ♗e4 57 ♘d2
♘×d2 58 ♖b6+ ♔f7 59 ♖b7+
♔f8 60 ♖b8+ ♔e7 61 ♖b7+
♔e8 62 ♔×d2 ♖×h4 63 ♘c3 d4
64 ♘×e4 ♖×e4 65 ♖g7 ♖×e3 66
♖×g6 0–1

46 Korchnoi–Reshevsky
Candidates' Match (4) 1968

1 ♘f3 ♘f6 2 g3 d5 3 ♗g2 c6 4 b3
♗f5 5 ♗b2 e6 6 0–0 ♗e7 7 d3 h6 8
♘bd2 0–0 9 ♕e1 ♘bd7 10 e4 ♗h7
11 ♕e2 a5 12 a4 ♕b6 13 e5 ♘e8 14
♗h3 ♘c7 15 ♔h1 ♖ae8 16 ♘h4
f6 17 ef ♗×f6 18 ♗×f6 ♖×f6 19 f4
♕c5 20 ♘df3 ♕c3 21 ♗g4 d4 22
♘e5 ♘×e5 23 fe ♖×f1+ 24 ♖×f1
♕c5 25 ♕f2 ♖f8 26 ♕×f8+ ♕×f8
27 ♖×f8+ ♔×f8 28 ♘f3 c5 29
♘d2 ♘d5 30 ♘c4(*46*)

30 . . . ♘b4? 31 ♘×a5 ♘×c2 32
♘×b7 c4 33 bc ♗×d3 34 ♘c5
♗×c4 35 ♗×e6 ♗×e6 36 ♘×e6+
♔e7 37 ♘c5 ♘b4 38 a5 ♘c6 39 a6
♔d8 40 ♔g2 g6 41 e6 ♔e7 42 ♔f3
♔d6 43 ♔e4 g5 44 g4 1–0

47 Tal–Korchnoi
Candidates' Match (5) 1968

1 e4 e5 2 ♘f3 ♘c6 3 ♗b5 a6 4 ♗a4
♘f6 5 0–0 ♗e7 6 ♖e1 b5 7 ♗b3 d6
8 c3 0–0 9 h3 ♘a5 10 ♗c2 c5 11 d4
♕c7 12 ♘bd2 ♘c6 13 dc dc 14
♘f1 ♗e6 15 ♘e3 ♖ad8 16 ♕e2 c4
17 ♘f5 ♗×f5 18 ef ♖fe8 19 ♗g5
h6 20 ♗×f6 ♗×f6 21 ♘d2 ♘e7 22
♘e4 ♘d5 23 b3 ♘×c3 24 ♘×f6+
gf 25 ♕e3 cb 26 ♗×b3 ♔h7 27
♖ec1 b4 28 a3

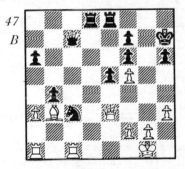

28 . . . e4 29 ab ♖d3 30 ♕e1 e3 31
♗c2 ♖d2 32 fe ♘e2+ 33 ♔h1
♘g3+ 34 ♔g1 ♖e2 35 ♕d1 ♕b7
36 e4 ♖8×e4 0–1

48 Korchnoi–Spassky
Candidates' Match (6) 1968

1 d4 d5 2 c4 e6 3 ♘c3 ♗e7 4 cd ed 5

♗f4 c6 6 ♕c2 g6 7 0-0-0 ♘f6 8 f3
♘a6 9 e4 ♘b4 10 ♕b3 ♗e6 11 e5
♘d7 12 a3 a5 13 ab ab 14 ♘b1 c5
15 g4 c4 16 ♕e3 ♖a2 17 h4 ♕a5 18
♖h2 ♖a1 19 ♗d3 b3 20 ♘e2 ♗b4
21 h5 0-0 22 hg fg 23 ♖dh1 cd 24
♕×d3 ♕c7+

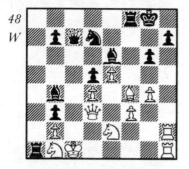

48
W

25 ♘c3 ♘b6 26 ♕×g6+ hg 27
♖h8+ ♔f7 28 ♖1h7+ ♔e8 29
♖×f8+ ♔×f8 30 ♖×c7 ♘c4 31
♖×b7 ♗×c3 32 bc b2+ 33 ♔c2
♔e8 34 ♗g5 ♖a6 35 ♘d2 ♗c8 36
♖e7+ ♔f8 37 ♘×c4 dc 38 ♔×b2
♖b6+ 39 ♔c2 ♗b7 40 ♖×b7
♖×b7 41 f4 ♖h7 42 ♔b2 1-0

49 Larsen–Korchnoi
Palma de Mallorca 1968

1 c4 c5 2 ♘c3 ♘f6 3 ♘f3 d5 4 cd
♘×d5 5 e3 e6 6 d4 ♘c6 7 ♗d3
♗e7 8 0-0 0-0 9 a3 ♘×c3 10 bc
♗f6 11 ♖b1 g6 12 ♗e4 ♕c7 13 a4
b6 14 a5 ♗a6 15 ab ab 16 ♖e1
♖a7 17 h4 ♘a5 18 h5 ♖d8 19
♘d2 ♗g7 20 hg hg 21 ♕f3 ♘c4 22
♘×c4 ♗×c4 23 ♖d1 b5 24 ♗d2
♖a2 25 ♗c6 ♕a5 26 ♕g4 ♗d3 27
♖bc1 ♗c2 28 ♖e1 cd 29 ed ♗×d4
30 ♕g5 ♗×f2+ 31 ♔×f2 ♖×d2+
32 ♔g1 ♕×c3 33 ♕×b5 ♕d4+ 34
♔h1 ♕h4+ 35 ♔g1

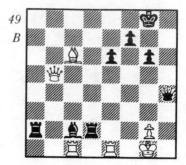

49
B

35 ... ♗e4 36 ♕b8+ ♔h7 37
♗×e4 ♖×g2+ 38 ♗×g2 ♕f2+ 39
♔h2 ♕×g2 mate

50 Korchnoi–Spassky
Palma de Mallorca 1968

1 d4 ♘f6 2 c4 e6 3 ♘f3 b6 4 g3 ♗b7
5 ♗g2 ♗b4+ 6 ♗d2 a5 7 0-0
♗×d2 8 ♕×d2 0-0 9 ♘c3 ♘e4 10
♘×e4 ♗×e4 11 ♘h4 ♗×g2 12
♘×g2 d6 13 ♖ad1 ♘d7 14 e4
♕b8 15 ♕e2 a4 16 ♘e3 ♕b7 17
♘c2 ♖fe8 18 ♖fe1 ♖a5 19 ♘a3
c6 20 ♕c2 b5 21 cb cb 22 ♖c1 b4
23 ♘c4 ♖a6 24 ♕d2 d5 25 ed
♕×d5 26 ♕×b4 ♘f6 27 ♕c5 h6 28
♕×d5 ♘×d5 29 a3 ♖b8 30 ♖c2
g5 31 ♔f1 ♔g7 32 ♘e5 ♖ab6 33
♖ee2 ♖6b7 34 ♔e1 h5 35 ♘d3
♔f6

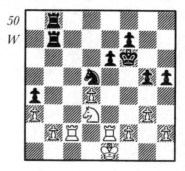

50
W

36 ♘c5 ♖a7 37 ♖c4 ♖ba8 38
♘e4+ ♔g6 39 ♘c3 ♘e7 40 ♔d2
♘f5 41 ♔c1 ♖d8 42 ♖×a4 ♖×a4
43 ♘×a4 ♘×d4 44 ♖e3 ♔f5 45 h3
h4 46 gh gh 47 b4 e5 48 ♘c3 ♔e6
49 ♘e2 ♘×e2+ 50 ♖×e2 f5 51 b5
♖a8 52 b6 ♔d6 53 ♖b2 ♔c6 54
b7 ♖b8 55 ♔d2 1–0

51 Korchnoi–Mecking
Palma de Mallorca 1969

1 d4 ♘f6 2 c4 e6 3 ♘c3 ♗b4 4 e3
0–0 5 ♘f3 c5 6 ♗e2 b6 7 0–0 ♗b7 8
♘a4 cd 9 ed ♗e7 10 a3 ♘e4 11 d5
b5 12 cb ♗×d5 13 ♗e3 f5 14 ♖c1
♕e8 15 ♖c1 g5 16 ♗d3 g4

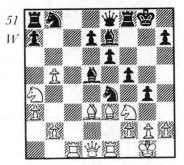

17 ♗×c4 ♗×e4 18 ♘d2 ♗d5 19
♗f4 ♗f6 20 ♘c3 ♗×c3 21 bc a6
22 c4 ♗b7 23 ♗d6 ♖f6 24 ♘b3 ab
25 cb ♕h5 26 ♖c7 ♗d5 27 ♖c8+
♔g7 28 ♕d4 ♗×b3 29 ♗e7 e5 30
♗×f6+ ♔×f6 31 ♕×e5+ ♔g6 32
♖×b8 1–0

52 Korchnoi–Karpov
38th USSR Ch. 1970

1 c4 c5 2 ♘f3 ♘f6 3 ♘c3 d5 4 cd
♘×d5 5 d4 cd 6 ♕×d4 ♘×c3 7
♕×c3 ♘c6 8 e4 a6 9 ♗c4 ♕a5 10
♗d2 ♕×c3 11 ♗×c3 e6 12 0–0

♖g8 13 ♖fd1 b5 14 ♗d3 f6 15 a4
b4 16 ♗d4 ♘×d4 17 ♘×d4 ♗c5
18 ♗c4 ♗×d4 19 ♖×d4 ♔e7

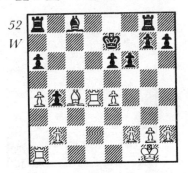

20 ♖ad1 ♖a7 21 b3 a5 22 ♖d6
♗d7 23 f4 ♖c8 24 e5 fe 25 fe ♖c5
26 ♖e1 h6 27 h4 ♖a8 28 ♖e3 ♖c6
29 ♖d4 ♖c5 30 ♖d6 ♖c6 31
♖×c6 ♗×c6 32 ♖g3 ♖g8 33 ♔f2
g5 34 ♔e3 g4 35 ♔d4 h5 36 ♔c5
♗e4 37 ♔b6 ♖a8 38 ♗d3 ♗f5 39
♖e3 ♖c8 40 ♗c4 ♗c2 41 ♔b5
♖a8 42 ♖e2 ♗g6 43 g3 ♗f5 44
♖d2 ♗e4 45 ♖d6 ♗d5 46 ♗×d5
ed 47 ♖×d5 ♔e6 48 ♖c5 ♖a7 49
♔b6 ♖d7 50 ♔×a5 ♖d3 51
♔×b4 ♖×g3 52 a5 ♖g1 53 ♖c2
g3 54 ♖a2 ♖h1 55 a6 ♖×h4+ 56
♔c3 ♖h3 57 ♖g2 1–0

53 Korchnoi–Hübner
Wijk aan Zee 1971

1 c4 g6 2 d4 ♗g7 3 ♘c3 d6 4 e4 e5 5
♘f3 ♗g4 6 d5 a5 7 ♗e2 ♘a6 8 0–0
♘e7 9 a3 0–0 10 ♖b1 c5 11 ♗d2
♗d7 12 ♘b5 ♘c8 13 b3 h6 14 g3
♘c7 15 ♘h4 ♘×b5 16 cb ♘e7 17
b4 cb 18 ab a4 19 ♖a1 f5 20 ef gf 21
♘g2 ♘×f5 22 ♗e3 ♘×e3 23 fe
♖×f1+ 24 ♗×f1 ♕f6 25 e4 ♖f8
26 ♕d2 ♕f3 27 ♗d3 ♗f6 28 ♘e1
♕h5 29 ♗e2 ♕g6 30 ♕e3 ♖a8 31

♞c2 ♝d8 32 ♝d3 ♛e8 33 ♞a3
♝h3 34 ♝e2 ♛d7 35 ♚h1 ♜c8 36
♞c4 ♜a8 37 ♜g1 ♛×b5 38 g4

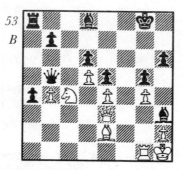

53
B

38 ... ♛×b4? 39 ♛×h3 ♚g7 40
♛f3 ♝e7 41 ♞e3 1–0

54 Korchnoi–Geller
Candidates' Match (5) 1971

1 d4 d5 2 c4 e6 3 ♞c3 ♝e7 4 ♞f3
♞f6 5 ♝g5 0–0 6 e3 h6 7 ♝h4 b6 8
♝e2 ♝b7 9 ♝×f6 ♝×f6 10 cd ed
11 0–0 ♛e7 12 ♛b3 ♜d8 13 ♜ad1
c5 14 dc ♝×c3 15 ♛×c3 bc 16
♜c1 ♞d7 17 ♜c2 ♜ab8 18 b3
♛e6 19 ♜d1 ♛b6

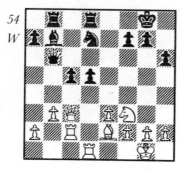

54
W

20 ♞e1 ♜bc8 21 ♝g4 ♛g6 22
♝h3 ♜c7 23 ♞d3 ♞f6 24 ♛a5
♞e8 25 ♜×c5 ♜×c5 26 ♞×c5 1–0

55 R. Byrne–Korchnoi
Moscow 1971

1 e4 c5 2 ♞f3 d6 3 d4 cd 4 ♞×d4
♞f6 5 ♞c3 a6 6 ♝e3 ♞bd7 7 g4 d5
8 g5 ♞×e4 9 ♞×e4 de 10 ♞b3 b6
11 ♛d4 ♝b7 12 0–0–0 ♛c7 13
♝g2 e5 14 ♛a4 ♜c8 15 ♜d2 ♛c6
16 ♛×c6 ♝×c6 17 ♜hd1 ♝e7 18
h4 h6 19 ♝h3 ♜d8 20 gh gh 21 h5
♞f6 22 ♝×b6 ♜×d2 23 ♞×d2
♞×h5 24 ♝f5 ♝g5 25 ♚b1 ♝×d2
26 ♜×d2 ♚e7 27 ♝c7

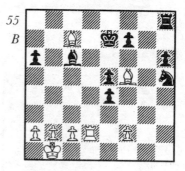

55
B

27 ... ♜g8 28 c4 ♚f6 29 ♝h3 ♞f4
30 ♜d6+ ♚g5 31 ♝f1 ♚f5 32
♜×c6 ♜g1 33 ♜×h6 ♜×f1+ 34
♚c2 ♜×f2+ 35 ♚c3 e3 36 ♝b6
♚e4 37 ♜h1 ♞e2+ 38 ♚b4 ♞d4
39 ♚a3 f5 40 ♝a5 f4 0–1

56 Korchnoi–Spassky
Moscow 1971

1 ♞f3 d5 2 c4 e6 3 g3 ♞f6 4 ♝g2
♝e7 5 0–0 0–0 6 d4 c6 7 ♛c2
♞bd7 8 b3 b6 9 ♜d1 ♝b7 10 ♞c3
b5 11 cb cb 12 ♞×b5 ♛a5 13 a4
♞e4 14 ♞d2 ♜ac8 15 ♛a2 a6 16
♝×e4 de

17 ♞c4 ♜×c4 18 bc ab 19 ab ♛c7
20 c5 ♝d5 21 ♛a7 ♛d8 22 c6 ♞f6
23 ♝a3 ♝×a3 24 ♜×a3 ♝c4 25

b6 e3 26 ♖×e3 ♘d5 27 b7 ♘×e3
28 fe ♕g5 29 d5 ♗×e2 1–0

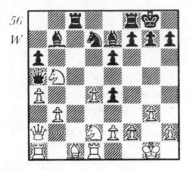

57 Tal–Korchnoi
Moscow 1971

1 e4 e6 2 d4 d5 3 ♘d2 c5 4 ♘gf3
♘c6 5 ♗b5 cd 6 ♘×d4 ♗d7 7
♘×c6 bc 8 ♗d3 ♕c7 9 ♕e2 ♘e7 10
♘f3 ♘g6 11 e5 ♖b8 12 0–0 ♗e7
13 ♖e1 c5 14 c4 0–0 15 h4

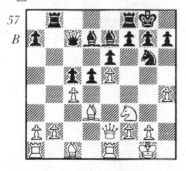

15 ... dc 16 ♗e4 ♔h8 17 ♗g5
♗d5 18 ♕e3 ♖fd8 19 h5 ♗×g5 20
♘×g5 ♘f8 21 ♖ad1 h6 22 ♘f3
♘d7 23 ♕f4 f5 24 ♗c2 ♘f6 25
♖d6 ♘d5 26 ♕g3 ♖b6 27
♖×d8+ ♕×d8 28 ♖d1 ♗e8 29 b3
cb 30 ♗×b3 ♗×h5 31 ♖c1 ♖b4
32 ♗c4 ♗×f3 33 ♕×f3 ♕g5 34
♕d1 ♕f4 35 ♗×d5 ♖d4 36 ♕c2

♖×d5 37 ♖e1 ♖×e5 38 ♖×e5
♕×e5 39 ♕a4 ♕e1+ 40 ♔h2
♕×f2 0–1

58 Korchnoi–Karpov
Hastings 1971–72

1 d4 ♘f6 2 ♘f3 e6 3 ♗g5 b6 4 e4 h6
5 ♗×f6 ♕×f6 6 ♗d3 ♗b7 7 ♘bd2
a6 8 ♕e2 d6 9 0–0–0 ♘d7 10 ♔b1
e5 11 c3 ♗e7 12 ♘c4 0–0 13 ♗c2
♖fe8 14 d5 c5 15 ♘e3 ♗f8 16 g4
♕d8 17 g5 h5

18 g6 fg 19 ♖hg1 ♕f6 20 ♘g5 ♗e7
21 ♘e6 ♘f8 22 ♘c7 ♕f7 23 ♖df1
b5 24 ♘×a8 ♗×a8 25 c4 ♖b8 26
♗d3 ♕e8 27 ♖c1 ♗f6 28 ♖g2
♖b6 29 ♖cg1 ♖b8 30 ♕f1 b4 31
♗e2 h4 32 ♖×g6 ♕×g6 33 ♖×g6
♘×g6 34 ♗g4 ♘f4 35 ♕d1 b3 36
ab ♗b7 37 ♘g2 ♗c8 38 ♗×c8
♖×c8 39 ♕g4 ♖e8 40 ♘×f4 ef 41
♕×f4 ♗e5 42 ♕×h4 ♖f8 43 b4
♗d4 44 bc 1–0

59 Uhlmann–Korchnoi
Skopje Olympiad 1972

1 c4 c5 2 ♘f3 ♘f6 3 ♘c3 d5 4 cd
♘×d5 5 ♕a4+ ♘c6 6 ♘e5 ♕c7 7
♘×d5 ♕×e5 8 ♘b6 ♖b8 9 ♘×c8
♖×c8 10 e3 ♕d5 11 ♕g4 e6 12 b3

h5 13 ♕h3 ♖d8 14 ♗c4 ♕e5 15
♖b1 ♕e4 16 ♖b2 ♗c7 17 d3 ♕g6
18 ♗b5 0–0 19 ♗×c6

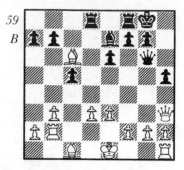

59
B

19 . . . ♕×d3 20 ♖d2 ♕c3 21 ♔e2
bc 22 ♖hd1 ♖×d2+ 23 ♗×d2
♕c2 24 ♕×h5 ♖d8 25 ♕g4 ♕×a2
26 ♕a4 ♕c2 27 ♕×a7 ♗f6 28
♕a5 ♖d5 29 ♖c1 ♕d3+ 30 ♔e1
c4 31 ♕b4 c5 0–1

60 Korchnoi–Ciocaltea
Skopje Olympiad 1972

1 d4 ♘f6 2 c4 g6 3 ♘c3 ♗g7 4 g3
0–0 5 ♗g2 d6 6 ♘f3 ♘c6 7 0–0
♗g4 8 d5 ♘a5 9 b3 c5 10 ♗b2 a6
11 ♕c2 ♖b8 12 ♘d2 b5 13 ♖fe1
♕c7 14 ♘d1 ♖b7 15 ♗c3 ♖fb8
16 f4 bc 17 bc ♘e8 18 ♘f2 ♗d7 19
♘d3 ♖a7 20 ♗×g7 ♘×g7 21 ♕c3
♘b7 22 e4 ♕a5 23 ♕b2 ♖aa8 24

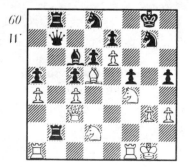

60
H

♘b3 ♕d8 25 ♕c3 a5 26 a4 ♕c7 27
♘d2 ♘d8 28 h3 h5 29 f5 gf 30 e5
♖a7 31 ♘f4 ♖ab7 32 e6 fe 33 de
♗c6 34 ♗d5 ♖b2 35 ♖f1 ♕b7(60)
   36 ♘×h5 ♘×h5 37 ♖×f5 ♘f6
38 ♖g5+ ♔h8 39 ♖f1 ♖×d2 40
♕×d2 1–0

61 Tukmakov–Korchnoi
Leningrad Interzonal 1973

1 d4 ♘f6 2 c4 e6 3 g3 d5 4 ♗g2 dc 5
♘f3 b5 6 a4 c6 7 0–0 ♗b7 8 ♘e5 a6
9 b3 cb 10 ♗b2 ♕b6 11 ♕×b3
♘bd7 12 ♘×d7 ♘×d7 13 ♘d2
♗e7 14 d5 cd 15 ♗×g7 ♖g8 16
♗c3 ♖g4 17 ♖fb1 ♗c5 18 e3

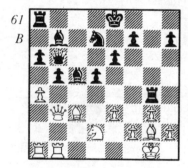

61
B

18 . . . ♗×e3 19 fe ♕×e3+ 20 ♔h1
♖c8 21 ♗a5 ♕×b3 22 ♘×b3
♖×a4 23 ♖×a4 ba 24 ♘d2 ♗c6
25 ♖c1 ♘e5 26 ♔g1 ♔d7 27 ♘f3
♘×f3+ 28 ♗×f3 d4 29 ♗h5 f5 30
g4 fg 31 ♖d1 ♗d5 32 ♖×d4
♖c1+ 33 ♔f2 a3 34 ♗×g4 a2 35
♗c3 ♖c2+ 36 ♔e1 ♖×c3 37
♖×d5+ ♔e7 38 ♖d1 ♖b3 0–1

62 Korchnoi–R. Byrne
Leningrad Interzonal 1973

1 d4 ♘f6 2 c4 g6 3 ♘c3 ♗g7 4 e4
d6 5 ♘f3 0–0 6 ♗e2 e5 7 0–0 ♘c6 8

d5 ♘e7 9 ♗d2 c5 10 dc bc 11 ♗g5
♗e6 12 c5 ♘e8 13 cd ♘×d6 14
♕a4 f6 15 ♗e3 ♕c7 16 ♖ac1
♖fb8 17 ♖fd1 ♗f8 18 ♖d2 ♘ec8

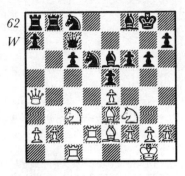

62
W

19 ♘d5 ♕f7 20 ♕×c6 ♘×e4 21
♘×f6+ ♘×f6 22 ♘g5 ♗d7 23
♕a6 ♕e7 24 ♗c5 ♕g7 25 ♕c4+
♔h8 26 ♘f7+ ♔g8 27 ♘×e5+
♔h8 28 ♗×f8 1-0

63 Larsen-Korchnoi
Leningrad Interzonal, 1973
English Opening

In the career of such a famous
tournament fighter as Larsen, the
Interzonal Tournament was by no
means one of his most striking
pages. After making an excellent
start, he could not maintain the
tempo set first by him, and then by
his rivals. Being a true sportsman,
Larsen does not like to complain of
subjective causes. But in fact, just
before the tournament he had been
on a diet, had begun to lose weight,
and had (thoughtlessly) continued
this during the tournament. In the
middle of the tournament, misfortunes began to beset him, and they
all began with the following game.

1 c4 e5 2 g3
The normal continuation is 2
♘c3. With the move in the game,
White prevents the manoeuvre
♗b4 with the eventual exchange of
this bishop for his queen's knight.
However, with 2 g3 the exerting of
pressure on the centre is essentially
delayed, and Black exploits this
hesitation to strengthen his position
in the centre.
2 ... c6 3 ♘f3 e4 4 ♘d4 d5 5 cd
♕×d5!
According to analysis by Keres,
Black is supposed to capture on d5
with his pawn – immediately, or
after the preliminary 5 ... ♘f6 6
♘c3 ♕b6 7 ♘b3. Although as
White against Keres I had twice
failed to gain any tangible
advantage, I preferred to capture
on d5 with my queen, especially
since in my preparations I had
spent much time on the analysis of
this position.
6 ♘b3
Or 6 ♘c2 ♘f6 7 ♗g2 ♕h5 8 h3
♕g6 9 ♘c3 ♗d6, with a good
game for Black, as occurred in the
game Shamkovich-Baumbach,
Moscow 1970.
6 ... ♘f6 7 ♗g2 ♕h5 8 h3
8 ♘c3 would, of course, have
been answered by 8 ... ♗h3,
exchanging off White's important
bishop. Analysing this game, I.
Zaitsev suggests here 8 ♕c2, and
reckons that this give White the
advantage. But on 8 ♕c2, 8 ...
♗h3 is again possible. After 9
♗×e4 ♘×e4 10 ♕×e4+ ♗e7 11
♘c3 ♘d7 Black has compensation
for the sacrificed pawn. Also
possible is 8 ... ♗f5 9 ♘d4 ♗g6 10

♕b3 b6, when White has achieved little.

8 ... ♕g6 9 ♘c3 ♘bd7

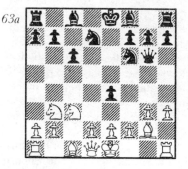

63a

At the cost of a certain weakening of his central pawn at e4, Black has gained the possibility of free development for his pieces, and a slight, though temporary, advantage in space. But he must keep an eye on his 'e' pawn. At the board I, for a long time, was unable to chose between 9 ... ♘bd7 and 9 ... ♘a6. The point of moving the knight to a6 is that 10 ♕c2 would then be dangerous for White, on account of the reply 10 ... ♘b4. As later games have shown, another good continuation here is 9 ... ♗b4, aiming to develop the K-side as quickly as possible.

10 ♕c2

This move leads to a position of approximate equality. White had other possibilities at his disposal, involving, in particular, the idea of undermining and exchanging off the pawn at e4, and then replacing it with his own, white pawn, thus seizing the centre. I naturally considered this possibility at the board, and worked out the following variation: 10 0–0 ♗d6 11

d3 ed. 12 e4 ♘e5 13 f4 ♕×g3 14 fe ♗×e5, when I reckoned that for the sacrificed piece Black has three pawns plus an attack. Indeed, after 15 ♖f3 ♕h2+ 16 ♔f1 ♘h5 17 ♕×d3 ♘g3+ 18 ♔f2 ♘h1+ the game must end in a draw, while after 17 ♖×d3 ♘g3+ 18 ♔f2 ♗×h3 19 ♕g1 the resulting endgame looks slightly favourable for White, but that is all. As we see, active piece play saves Black, although it must be admitted that his position hangs by a thread.

10 ... e3 11 ♕×g6

White must exchange queens, otherwise his king, which will soon find itself on f2, will come under attack.

11 ... ef+ 12 ♔×f2 hg 13 d4

The first impression is that White, with his pawn centre, has a clear advantage. But in fact the pawn centre which White now sets up is not only a strength in White's position – he will soon be forced to defend it. Therefore the unhurried 13 d3 deserved consideration.

13 ... ♘b6 14 e4 ♗e6 15 ♗f4 ♗b4 16 ♘c5

This looks very powerful; in the event of 16 ... ♗×c5 17 dc ♘bd7 18 ♗d6 Black's position is very cramped.

16 ... 0–0–0!

It turns out that in this position the two bishops are not that important, whereas along the 'f' file Black can create threats against the enemy king.

17 ♘×e6 fe 18 a3 ♗e7 19 ♖ad1 ♖hf8

By 19 ... ♘c4 Black could have already won a pawn, e.g. 20 ♗c1

♖xd4! 21 ♖xd4 ♗c5 22 ♖hd1 e5 23 ♗43 ♘xe3, with advantage to Black. This is probably what I should have played, but I didn't want the critics to accuse me of a recurrence of my old weakness (pawn-grabbing!). And indeed, in winning a pawn I could have lost the initiative. By intuition I made the move which seemed to increase Black's threats.

20 ♔e2

In the event of 20 ♗f3 the variation 20 ... ♘c4 21 ♗c1 ♖xd4 or 21 ... e5 would gain in strength.

20 ... ♘c4 21 h4!

On 21 ♗c1, 21 ... ♘h5 would be unpleasant, and after 22 ♖d3 c5! 23 d5 ♗d6 Black has the advantage (this variation was pointed out by I. Zaitsev). Now White threatens the highly unpleasant 22 ♗h3.

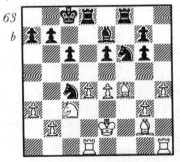

63
b

21 ... ♘h5! 22 ♗h3 ♖xf4

This exchange sacrifice is forced, but at the same time it is highly unpleasant for White, whose king becomes the object of attack.

23 ♗xe6+?!

But nervertheless the sacrifice should have been accepted! After 23 gf ♘xf4+ 24 ♔f3 ♖f8 25 ♔g3,

despite the many tempting attacks and checks, Black has nothing decisive. Thus, for instance, Zaitsev gives the variation 25 ... ♘e3 26 ♖d2 ♘xh3 27 ♖e2! ♗xh4+!? 28 ♔xh4 ♘f4 29 ♖xe3 ♘g2+ 30 ♔g5 ♘xe3 31 ♔xg6, with a draw. Black would probably have had to play 25 ... ♘xb2 26 ♖df1 ♘bd3 – with material approximately level, Black has a slight initiative.

23 ... ♔c7 24 ♗xc4 ♘xg3+ 25 ♔e3 ♖df8

Black strives to create as many threats as possible to the enemy king; the winning of the 'h' pawn will not by itself win the game for Black.

26 ♖hg1 ♗xh4 27 ♔d3 ♖f2 28 ♖d2 ♗g5! 29 ♖xf2 ♖xf2 30 ♘e2

In defending against the mate, White loses his 'e' pawn. Things were equally unpleasant for him after other moves, e.g. 30 ♗f7!? ♖d2+ 31 ♔c4 ♗f4 32 b4 b5+, winning the 'd' pawn.

30 ... ♖f3+ 31 ♔c2 ♘xe4 32 ♗d3 ♖e3 33 ♘c3

Or 33 ♖g4 ♖xd3, with a winning position for Black.

33 ... ♘g3 34 d5 ♗f6 35 ♘d1 ♖f3 36 dc ♔xc6 37 ♗xg6 ♔d6 38 ♖e1 ♘f5 39 ♖e8 ♘d4+ 40 ♔d2 ♗g5+ 41 ♔e1 ♗h4+ 42 ♔d2 ♖g3

Despite his extra pawn and the activity of his pieces, Black would still have had to demonstrate good technique in order to win, if White had played 43 ♗d3. But there followed

43 ♗e4? ♗g5+

and, since he loses a piece, White resigned.

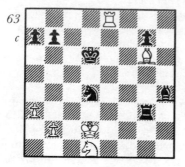

63
c

64 Korchnoi–Hübner
Leningrad Interzonal 1973

1 c4 ♘f6 2 ♘c3 c5 3 ♘f3 g6 4 e4
♗g7 5 d4 cd 6 ♘×d4 ♘c6 7 ♘c2
d6 8 ♗e2 ♘d7 9 ♗d2 ♘c5 10 b4
♘e6 11 ♖c1 0–0 12 ♘d5 ♘ed4 13
♘×d4 ♘×d4 14 ♗g5 ♖e8 15 0–0
♗e6 16 ♖e1 ♘×e2+ 17 ♖×e2
♕d7 18 ♖d2 ♗×d5 19 ♖×d5 ♕e6
20 ♕d3 ♖ac8 21 ♗e3 a6 22 h3
♖f8 23 g4 ♕f6 24 ♗g5 ♕b2 25 a3
♖c7 26 c5 ♖fc8 27 ♔g2 ♗f8

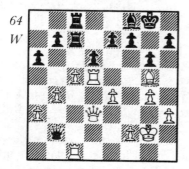

64
W

28 cd ed 29 ♖×c7 ♖×c7 30 e5
♖c2 31 ♗d2 de 32 ♖d8 ♔g7 33 ♕e3
♗e7 34 ♕h6+ ♔f6 35 ♕h4+
♔e6 36 ♖e8 ♖×d2 37 ♕×e7+
♔d5 38 ♖d8+ ♔c6 1–0

65 Korchnoi–Smyslov
41st USSR Ch. 1973

1 e4 e5 2 ♘f3 ♘c6 3 ♗b5 a6 4 ♗a4
♘f6 5 0–0 ♗e7 6 ♖e1 b5 7 ♗b3
0–0 8 c3 d6 9 h3 ♘a5 10 ♗c2 c5 11
d4 ♕c7 12 ♘bd2 ♖e8 13 b3 ♗f8
14 ♘f1 g6 15 ♗g5 ♗g7 16 ♕d2 cd
17 cd ed 18 ♘×d4 ♘c6 19 ♘×c6
♕×c6 20 ♘g3 ♗b7 21 ♖ac1
♖ac8 22 ♗b1 ♕b6 23 ♗e3 ♕d8

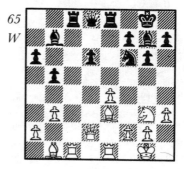

65
W

24 ♖×c8 ♕×c8 25 ♕×d6 ♘×e4
26 ♗×e4 ♗×e4 27 ♖c1 ♕a8 28
♘×e4 ♖×e4 29 ♕d7 ♖e8 30
♖c7 ♖f8 31 ♖a7 ♕e4 32 ♖×a6
♗e5 33 ♖c6 ♕b1+ 34 ♖c1 ♕×a2
35 ♕×b5 ♕b2 36 ♕d3 ♖a8 37
♕b1 ♕a3 38 b4 ♕a4 39 b5 ♗d4
40 ♗×d4 ♕×d4 41 b6 ♖b8 42
♖c6 ♖b7 43 ♕b3 ♔g7 44 g3 ♖e7
45 ♕f3 ♖e1+ 46 ♔g2 ♖e5 47
♕f6+ ♔h6 48 b7 ♕d5+ 49 ♕f3
♕b5 50 ♕f4+ ♔g7 51 ♖b6 1–0

66 Hübner–Korchnoi
1st match game Solingen 1973

1 ♘f3 ♘f6 2 c4 g6 3 ♘c3 d5 4 cd
♘×d5 5 g3 ♗g7 6 ♗g2 e5 7 0–0
♘e7 8 d3 ♘bc6 9 ♗d2 0–0 10 ♖c1
♘d4 11 ♘×d4 ed 12 ♘e4 h6 13
♕b3 b6 14 ♕c4 c6 15 ♗b4 ♗d7 16

♕a6 c5 17 ♗a3 ♗c8 18 ♕a4 a5 19 ♕c2 ♘d5 20 ♖ce1 ♖e8 21 b3 ♖a7 22 ♗b2 ♖ae7 23 ♕d1 f5 24 ♘d2 b5 25 ♗×d5 ♕×d5 26 f3 a4 27 ♖f2 ♖a7 28 ♕c2 ♗e6 29 ♖b1 g5 30 ♗c1 a3 31 ♘f1 c4 32 bc bc 33 ♘d2 cd 34 ed ♕×a2 35 ♕×a2 ♗×a2 36 ♖a1

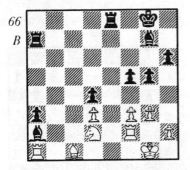

66 B

36 ... ♖c8 37 ♘f1 ♗d5 38 ♖×a3 ♖×a3 39 ♗×a3 ♖c3 40 ♗b2 ♖×d3 41 ♗d2 ♖×d2 42 ♘×d2 f4 43 gf gf 44 ♗c1 d3 45 ♔g2 ♔f7 46 ♘b1 ♗a2 47 ♘d2 ♗d4 48 ♘f1 ♗e5 49 ♘d2 ♗d5 50 ♘b1 ♔e6 51 ♗d2 h5 52 ♗b4 ♗d4 53 ♘d2 ♗e3 54 ♗c3 ♔f5 55 ♘f1 h4 56 ♘d2 ♔g6 57 ♗a5 ♗e6 58 ♘e4 h3+ 59 ♔f1 ♗d5 60 ♘d2 ♔f5 61 ♗c3 ♔e6 62 ♗b4 ♔d7 63 ♗c3 ♔d6 64 ♗b4+ ♔c6 65 ♗c3 ♔b5 66 ♔e1 ♗g1 67 ♘f1 ♗×f3 68 ♗d2 ♗e2 69 ♗×f4 ♗×f1 70 ♔×f1 ♗c5 71 ♗e1 ♔c4 72 ♔d2 ♗b4+ 73 ♔e3 ♔c3 74 ♔f2 ♔c2 0-1

67 Korchnoi–Mecking
Candidates' Match (13) 1974

1 d4 ♘f6 2 ♘f3 c5 3 d5 e6 4 c4 ed 5 cd d6 6 ♘c3 g6 7 e4 ♗g7 8 ♗e2 0-0 9 0-0 ♖e8 10 ♘d2 ♘bd7 11 ♕c2 ♘e5 12 b3 g5 13 ♗b2 g4 14 ♖fe1 ♘h5 15 ♘d1 ♗f4 16 ♗b5 ♖f8 17 ♘e3 ♗g5 18 ♘f5 ♗×f5 19 ef ♘ed3 20 ♗×d3 ♗×b2 21 ♖ad1

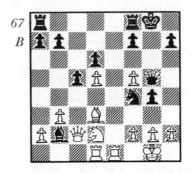

67 B

21 ... ♗d4? 22 ♘e4 ♕×f5 23 ♘g3 ♕g5 24 ♗×h7+ ♔h8 25 ♕f5 ♕h6 26 ♕×g4 ♘×g2 27 ♔×g2 ♕×h7 28 ♖e7 ♖g8 29 ♕f4 ♗e5 30 ♕f3 ♖g7 31 ♖×b7 ♕c2 32 ♖e1 ♔g8 33 ♖e4 ♖f8 34 ♖g4 ♕×a2 35 ♘f5 ♖×g4 36 ♕×g4+ ♔h7 37 ♕h5+ ♔g8 38 ♘h6+ ♔g7 39 ♘f7 ♖g8 40 ♘×e5+ ♔f6 41 ♘g4+ ♖×g4 42 ♕×g4 1-0

68 Korchnoi–Petrosian
Candidates' Match (1) Odessa 1974

1 c4 ♘f6 2 ♘c3 e6 3 ♘f3 b6 4 e4 ♗b7 5 d3 d6 6 g3 ♗e7 7 ♗g2 0-0 8 0-0 c5 9 b3 ♘a6 10 ♖e1 e5 11 ♗h3 ♘c7 12 ♘h4 g6 13 ♘g2 ♘e6 14 f4 ef 15 gf ♘h5 16 ♘d5 ♗f6 17 ♖b1 ♗d4+ 18 ♔h1 ♘c7 19 ♘de3 ♘g7 20 f5 ♘ce8 21 ♖f1 ♘f6 22 ♘c2 ♗e5 23 ♗g5 ♕e8 24 ♘ce3 ♔h8 25 ♕e1 ♘fh5 26 ♗g4 ♖g8 (68) 27 f6 ♘e6 28 ♕h4 ♘×g5 29 ♕×g5 ♗d4 30 ♗×h5 gh 31 ♕×h5 ♖g6 32 ♘f5 ♕e5 33 ♖f3 ♖×f6 34 ♖h3 h6 35 ♕g5 ♖e8? 36 ♕g7 mate

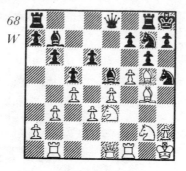

68
W

69 Korchnoi–Petrosian
Candidates' Match (3) 1974

1 c4 ♘f6 2 ♘c3 e6 3 ♘f3 b6 4 e4
♗b7 5 ♕e2 c5 6 e5 ♘g8 7 d4 ♗×f3
8 ♕×f3 ♘c6 9 d5 ♘×e5 10 ♕g3
d6 11 ♗f4 ♘g6 12 de fe 13 0-0-0
♘×f4 14 ♕×f4 g6

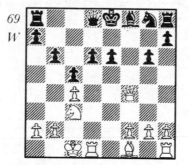

69
W

15 ♕e4 ♘f6 16 ♕×e6+ ♕e7 17
♖×d6 ♕×e6 18 ♖×e6+ ♔f7 19
♖c6 ♖c8 20 ♖×c8 ♗h6+ 21 ♔c2
♖×c8 22 ♗e2 ♖d8 23 ♔b3 ♖d2
24 ♖d1 ♘e8 25 ♖×d2 ♗×d2 26
♘b5 a6 27 ♘c3 ♗×c3 28 ♔×c3 a5
29 ♗d3 ♘f6 30 f4 ♘h5 31 g3 ♘f6
32 ♔d2 ♘e8 33 g4 ♘d6 34 ♔e3
♔e6 35 h4 ♔f7 36 b3 ♔g7 37 g5
♔f7 38 f5 gf 39 ♔f4 ♔g6 40 a4
♘e4 41 ♗×e4 fe 42 ♔×e4 ♔h5 43
♔f5 ♔×h4 44 g6 hg+ 45 ♔×g6
♔g4 46 ♔f6 ♔f4 47 ♔e6 ♔e4 48

♔d6 ♔d4 49 ♔c6 ♔c3 50 ♔×b6
♔×b3 51 ♔b5 1-0

70 Korchnoi–Petrosian
Candidates' Match (5) 1974
Sicilian Defence

1 c4 c5 2 ♘f3 ♘f6 3 ♘c3 g6 4 d4
cd 5 ♘×d4 ♗g7 6 e4 ♘c6 7 ♗e3
♘g4 8 ♕×g4 ♘×d4 9 ♕d1 ♘e6
10 ♕d2

This is not the first time that
Petrosian has played this system for
Black. Among the games that I can
at present recall are his victory over
Keres in the 1959 Candidates'
Tournament, and his loss to Larsen
at Santa Monica, 1966. Despite the
fact that Petrosian has a very varied
opening repertoire, I managed to
guess that it was this opening that
he would play. The day before the
game I spent several hours
analysing this opening system.

10 . . . d6 11 ♗e2

Here 11 ♖b1, with the idea of
playing b4, deserves consideration,
as occurred, for instance, in the
game Sanguinetti–Hübner, Biel
1976.

11 . . . ♕a5 12 ♖c1 ♗d7 13 0-0
♘c5 14 ♗h6!

The day before the game, it was
this position that I had studied with
my seconds, Osnos and Tseitlin!
Black is forced to exchange black-
squared bishops, and White has a
slight but persistent superiority,
based on his advantage in space.

14 . . . 0-0

14 . . . ♗×c3 fails to 15 ♖×c3
♘×e4 16 ♕d4 ♕e5 17 ♕×e5 de 18
♖e3 ♘f6 19 h3!, when White
regains his pawn, and with his two

bishops has the advantage in the ending.

15 ♗×g7 ♔×g7 16 b3!

This move hardly deserves an exclamation mark in itself. The point is that Petrosian – an admirer of Nimzowitsch – values prophylaxis in chess very highly, and is disconcerted by an opponent who also appreciates its merits. I recall that in the first game of the 1974 match I won the opening battle with the move 9 b3!

16 ... ♗c6 17 ♖fe1 ♘e6?!

More in the spirit of the opening system chosen by Black was 17 ... ♖ad8, with the idea of playing ... e5, and then transferring his knight to d4. But Petrosian, overrating his position, attempts to provoke weaknesses in the white position, without weakening his own pawn formation. Perhaps on 17 ... ♖ad8 Petrosian was afraid of 18 ♕b2, but forgot that after 18 ... e5 19 b4 he has the reply 19 ... ♕b6 – with an equal game.

18 ♗g4 ♖ad8 19 ♖e3

White has more space, but this does not mean that he can play without a plan, and still keep an advantage. 19 ♖cd1 was correct, with the intention of playing ♘d5, creating pressure on the black position down the central files.

19 ... ♘f4?!

Black should have played 19 ... ♕g5, especially since his queen no longer has anything to do on the Q-side. In the event of 20 ♗f5 ♘f4, the white king would feel rather uncomfortable with the enemy pieces hanging over him, while after 20 ♗×e6 fe 21 ♕d4+ ♕f6 22

♕×f6+ ef the resulting endgame would be level.

The operation undertaken by Black soon leads him into a difficult position.

20 g3 h5

In the event of 20 ... ♘h5 21 ♗×h5 ♕×h5 22 ♕d4+ Black loses his pawn at a7. Returning the knight to e6 is also not altogether satisfactory, in view of 21 ♕b2, when 22 ♘d5+ is threatened. Black could temporarily prevent this by 21 ... ♕e5, but then 22 f4 ♕d4 23 ♕f2 followed by ♖d1 and ♘d5 would give White a serious advantage.

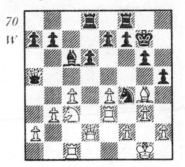

70
W

21 ♕b2!

I must admit that I did not find this move immediately. At first I considered the consequences of 21 gf hg followed by ♕h5, as well as 21 ♗f3 ♘h3+, and found that in every line Black stood better. Only then did the cunning intermediate move with the queen occur to me! Now Black does not succeed in switching his queen to the K-side, where things are happening, and his position becomes markedly inferior.

21 ... h×g4

If 21 . . . ♕g5, then 22 ♘d5+ e5
23 gf ♕×g4+ 24 ♖g3 ♕e6 25 f5,
with a clear advantage to White.

22 ♘d5+ e5 23 gf

At the board I was tempted to
resrict the black queen still further
by 23 b4, but unfortunately this
move doesn't work. By sacrificing
his queen: 23 . . . ♘×d5! 24 ba
♘×e3 25 fe ♗×e4 Black siezes the
initiative.

23 . . . ♖de8

Or 23 . . . ♗×d5 24 ed f6 25 ♖g3
ef 26 ♖×g4, and Black loses a
pawn.

24 ♖g3 ♗d7

At roughly this point, with an
hour to go before the time control,
Petrosian and I began our
'conversation', which did not
exactly accord with the FIDE code,
nor with the rules of conduct at the
chess board. Regarding this
conversation, the reader would do
best to refer to page 100 of my
autobiography.

More in the spirit of the
aggravated situation at the board
was 24 . . . f5, which would have
also have led to an exceptionally
sharp situation on the board itself.
However, as before the advantage
is with White . . .

25 ♖d1?

Here 25 ♘e3 was very strong,
with the idea of taking the pawn on
g4 with the knight. Then on 25 . . .
f5, either 26 ♖d1 or 26 c5 is very
strong. But it is not easy to play
when there is a 'heated argument'
going on . . .

25 . . . f6 26 fe ♖×e5?!

On this occasion it is Petrosian
who goes wrong. Black would have

had better drawing chances after 26
. . . fe 27 ♘e3 ♖f4 28 b4 ♕a4.

27 ♘c3

Now Black loses a pawn without
any compensation.

27 . . . ♕c5 28 ♕d2 f5

Or 28 . . . ♖e6 29 ♖×g4 f5 30
♖g5, when Black's position is very
depressing.

29 ♕×d6 ♕×d6 30 ♖×d6 Bc6
31 f3!

With the time scramble imminent, I succeeded in finding this
strong move. In his search for a
saving line, Petrosian used up
practically all of his time, but failed
to find a satisfactory defence. Most
probably, there no longer is one . . .

31 . . . ♔h6

If 31 . . . fe 32 fe ♗×e4, then
after 33 ♖e3 ♖fe8 34 ♘×e4 ♖×e4
35 ♖×e4 ♖×e4 36 ♖d7+, White
easily wins the ending. 31 . . . ♖f6
was suggested by the analysts as
being best. Then comes 32 ♖×f6
♔×f6 33 f4 ♖e8 34 e5+ ♔f7 35
♖e3. Now in the event of 35 . . .
♖d8 36 ♘d5! ♗×d5 37 ♖d3 ♔e6
38 cd+ ♖×d5 39 ♖×d5 ♔×d5 40
♔f2 b5 41 ♔g3 g5 42 fg ♔×e5 43
♔h4 f4 44 ♔×g4 ♔e4 45 g6 f3, a
queen ending results where it is
White to move and he is a pawn up.
No better is 35 . . . g5 36 fg f4 37
♖e1 ♔g6 38 e6 ♔×g5 39 ♘d5,
when White's 'e' pawn must win
the game for him. In the event of 31
. . . ♔h7 White would have played
32 fg fe 33 ♖e3 ♔h6 34 ♔g2 ♔g5
35 ♔g3, and again should
gradually win.

32 f4 ♖ee8 33 ef

White wins another pawn, and
were it not for the severe time

scramble, Black could already resign. But in time trouble anything can happen!

33 ... ♗f3 34 ♖×g6+ ♔h7

34 ... ♔h5 would have been answered by 35 h3! ♖×f5 36 hg+, winning a piece. Or 35 ... ♔h4 36 ♔h2 ♖×f5 37 hg, which is even more effective.

35 ♖g5 ♖e1+

On 35 ... ♖e3, 36 h3! again wins.

36 ♔f2 ♖h1

Again on 36 ... ♖c1 White wins by 37 h3!.

37 ♖h5+ ♔g7 38 ♘d5?

Here too White should have played 38 h3! – 38 ... ♖h2+ 39 ♔f1 ♖h1+ 40 ♖g1, and White wins. But in time trouble it seemed terrible to have to move the king onto the back rank! And – by the move in the game White seriously complicates the winning of the game . . .

38 ... ♖a1

White had reckoned only on 38 ... ♖e8, when after 39 ♘e3 Black loses his 'g' pawn.

39 f6+?!

Here again 39 h3 would have been simpler and stronger.

39 ... ♔g6 40 ♖g5+ ♔f7 41 ♖g7+ ♔e6 42 ♖c7+ ♔f5?

A rare instance in the practice of Petrosian. Normally he is accuracy itself, records the game in exemplary fashion, and after making 40 moves, immediately adjourns the game, since he trusts his analysis more than his play at the board. But on this occasion the score was forgotten! Following my example, Petrosian continued

playing at lightning speed! Meanwhile, by continuing 42 ... ♔d6 43 ♖×b7 ♖×a2+, Black could have caused his opponent considerable difficulties over the realization of his big material advantage. One further move was made:

43 ♖e5+

And at last Petrosian sealed the obvious

43 ... ♔g6

Analysis showed that, by playing 44 h3, White wins easily, so Petrosian did not turn up for the adjournament, and thus resigned the game.

71 Korchnoi–Karpov

Final Candidates' (21) Moscow 1974
Queen's Indian Defence

1 d4 ♘f6 2 ♘f3 e6 3 g3 b6 4 ♗g2 ♗b7 5 c4 ♗e7 6 ♘c3 0–0

As in the majority of the games from my match with Karpov where I was White, the Queen's Indian has been played. The opening phase is full of subtleties. If 6 ... ♘e4, then after 7 ♗d2, according to modern theory, White has a slight advantage. In the event of 7 0–0 ♘e4, theory considers that Black has better equalizing prospects. Has White a more useful move than castling? In a number of games I have played 7 ♕d3, but after 7 ... d5 it turns out that the white queen is on the wrong square . . .

I should add that, prior to this, the move 6 ... 0–0 had occurred only rarely in master games. It was essentially an opening preparation by Karpov for the match.

7 ♕c2

This is what I played in the 5th game of the match, but I was unhappy with the outcome of the opening, and so for a long time I did not revert to the queen move.

7 ... c5 8 d5 ed 9 ♘g5 ♘c6

In the fifth game Karpov played 9 ... g6, and obtained an excellent game from the opening, so that this knight move came as a surprise to me. Against 9 ... g6, I had spent several days in preparation, investigating the reply 10 h4!?, which leads to great complications.

On the whole I had several helpers during this match, but I prepared for this game with only one of my seconds (Bronstein!) – the others knew nothing about what and how I was planning to play. This was to be on the safe side – so that there should be no leakage of information!

To return to the position, I think that the best move here is neither 9 ... g6, nor, as was played, 9 ... ♘c6, but 9 ... ♘a6, temporarily preventing the occupation of d5 by one of White's minor pieces.

10 ♘xd5 g6 11 ♕d2!

Regarding this move, Botvinnik wrote in his book, *Three Matches of A. Karpov*: 'This strong move was most probably prepared by Korchnoi prior to the match'. Karpov said roughly the same thing in the press. But then how was I to know before the match which move order Karpov was going to choose – that he would castle on the sixth move! And what point was there in my looking at 9 ... ♘c6 and studying the resulting positions,

when I could see stronger moves for my opponent! I have great respect for both World Champions, but one gains the impression that neither of them could have found at the board this modest move, which defends the knight at g5, and places the queen on an important file.

11 ... ♘xd5

Karpov made this weak move after 8 minutes thought. But I repeat, this position was already in his theoretical notebook, and he was simply remembering what was written there. Meanwhile, the correct move, as pointed out by Botvinnik, was 11 ... ♖e8. In this case the exchange on e7 leaves Black with a big lead in development. Most probably White should play 12 ♘xf6+ ♗xf6 13 ♘e4, with a slight advantage, or perhaps 12 b3 would be quite good, with the intention of exchanging on e7 on the following move ...

12 ♗xd5 ♖b8?

The losing move, made after three minutes' thought. However, Black's position is, to put it mildly, rather depressing. Relatively best was 12 ... ♗xg5 13 ♕xg5 ♕xg5 14 ♗xg5, hoping to save the difficult ending.

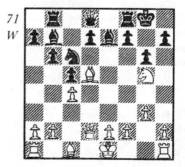

71
W

13 ♘×h7!

After the match, as is customary for a young genius, Karpov stated in the press that his loss in the 21st game was the fault of his seconds: they had missed this blow in their prepared analysis!

13... ♖e8

Or 13... ♔×h7 14 ♕h6+ ♔g8 15 ♕×g6+ ♔h8 16 ♕h6+ ♔g8 17 ♗e4 f5 18 ♗d5+ ♖f7 19 ♕g6+.

14 ♕h6 ♘e5 15 ♘g5 ♗×g5

After 15... ♗f6 16 ♗×f7+ White gives mate in three moves.

16 ♗×g5 ♕×g5 17 ♕×g5 ♗×d5

At this point I went up to the controller, and asked whether it was legal for me to castle when my rook was attacked. I was assured that it was. Afterwards, this incident was cited as being an indication of how extremely tired the players were. But in fact, out of the two and a half thousand games that I had played, there had never been an instance where it had been necessary for me to castle when my rook was attacked, and I was not sure that I understood correctly the rules of the game!

18 0-0!

If castling had been illegal, then White would still have had to work for his win; since 18 c×d5 would be fatal on account of 18... ♘f3+, he would have had to play 18 0-0-0.

18... ♗×c4 19 f4 Resigns.

72 Korchnoi–Petrosian
Moscow 1975

1 c4 ♘f6 2 ♘c3 e6 3 ♘f3 d5 4 d4 ♗e7 5 g3 0-0 6 ♗g2 ♘bd7 7 ♕d3 c6 8 0-0 b6 9 e4 ♗a6 10 b3 ♖c8 11 ♗f4 ♖e8 12 ♖fd1 ♘f8 13 a4 ♗b4 14 e5 ♘6d7 15 ♗d2 ♘b8 16 ♕c2 ♗e7 17 ♕a2 ♗b7 18 ♕b2 a5 19 h4 ♘a6 20 ♗g5 ♘b4 21 ♖ac1 ♖c7 22 ♕d2 ♕d7 23 ♘h2 ♗×g5 24 hg ♖ec8 25 ♘g4 ♕d8 26 f4 ♖d7 27 ♘e3 ♘g6 28 f5 ef 29 ♘×f5 ♘f8 30 ♘d6

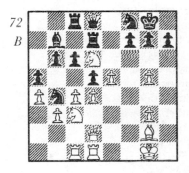

72
B

30... ♖×d6 31 ed ♕×d6 32 cd cd 33 ♕f4 ♕d8 34 ♗h3 ♘g6 35 ♕f3 ♖c6 36 ♖f1 ♖c7 37 ♘b5 ♖e7 38 ♖ce1 ♗a6 39 ♗f5 ♘f8 40 ♕f4 ♗×b5 41 ab ♖×e1 42 ♖×e1 g6 43 ♗b1 ♘e6 44 ♕f6 ♕c7 45 ♔g2 ♕c3 46 ♖f1 ♕c7 47 ♖f3 ♘f8 48 ♔f2 ♘e6 49 ♔e2 ♘g7 50 ♖e3 ♘e6 51 ♔d2 ♕d7 52 ♖c3 ♕c8 53 ♗c2 ♕f8 54 ♗b1 ♕e8 55 ♖f3 ♕f8 56 ♖f1 ♕e8 57 ♖f2 ♕f8 58 ♖f3 ♕g7 59 ♖c3 ♕f8 60 ♔c1 ♕e8 61 ♔b2 ♕a8 62 ♕e7 ♕b8 63 ♖f3 ♕f8 64 ♕f6 ♕e8 65 ♖c3 ♕a8 66 g4 ♕e8 67 ♕e5 ♕d8 68 ♗×g6 hg 69 ♖h3 ♘d3+ 70 ♖×d3 ♕×g5 71 ♖c3 ♘e4 72 ♖h3 f6 73 ♕h2 ♔f7 74 ♖h8 1-0

General Index

Index of Chess Players and Officials

(Page numbers in **bold** type refer to complete games)

Index of Games

(References to game nos. Italicised = Korchnoi White
bracketed page nos. where game is referred to in the text.)

Index of Game Openings

(References to game nos.)